A PASSION FOR POULTRY

GLUTEN SUGAR DAIRY FREE

MICHELLE E. DEBERGE

Dedication

I dedicate this book to all of the amazing people in the GSDF Community. To all of those who have had to keep a restricted diet due to medical or health reasons. To all of you that realize a restrictive diet does mean good, healthy food!

I dedicate this book to those that have felt overwhelmed, alone, frustrated and in physical pain due to food allergies or other medical illnesses that have you eating gluten, sugar and dairy free.

Our community at Gluten, Sugar, Dairy Free has continued to grow every week! We have a free membership that gives you weekly tips, videos and more all the way to paid support groups and much more.

At GSDF we are much more than just recipes, we are about education and we have classes every week and new ones created monthly.

Find our community here:

http://glutensugardairyfree.com/start-here

ACKNOWLEDGMENTS

-------MY PARTNER

I would like to acknowledge my partner who saw my passion for food, flavor profiles and writing recipes. He encouraged me to write all my recipes into new gluten, sugar, dairy free ones and built me the website to showcase them. That website turned into more than a recipe site as the community grew and we became an education and information site as well.

He supported me even when I got overwhelmed, doubted my ability to get everything done and always encourages me. His brilliant ideas of how to get this information out to those that most desperately need it has been invaluable. I am blessed to have him by my side, guiding me, supporting me and always being there no matter what or the miles that sometimes separate us. Because of him, I am able to follow my passion and for that I am grateful.

--------DR. JOHN DEWITT

I would like to acknowledge my friend and collaborator Dr. John DeWitt. Dr. John DeWitt has come aboard last year as the GSDF Health and Wellness Expert. He volunteers his time on The Artichoke Series teaching health and wellness and answering nutrition questions from the audience. John is always available to explain any medical questions I have or my clients have.

His work complements what we do here at GSDF. He is a partner in one of Southern California's most revered Health and Wellness Center where people travel from all over the world for treatment. Dr. DeWitt believes in the mind, body, spirit approach to health and wellness. He has just published another book called You Don't Need Your Glasses or Contacts: Natural Ways to Correct Your Vision Without Drugs or Corrective Lenses and has a new site called Relax to Clarity http://relaxtoclarity.com/ He also has another site http://drjohndewitt.com that has a whole section about GSDF and nutrition. I am thrilled with our collaboration and the community adores Dr. John when he joins us live!

--------JUSTIN AND KATE STELLMAN, EXTREME HEALTH RADIO

Justin and Kate Stellman are dear friends and we love to collaborate together. They are the founders and radio hosts of the very popular online radio show called Extreme Health Radio. They have interviewed over 300 alternative health professionals and share a wealth of information between the two of them.

Justin joins me on the GSDF Artichoke Series on a regular basis. We talk about how the balance of Mind, Body and Spirit works for optimal health. How to balance the three to achieve your health goals and discourage illness. He discusses how his personal practices have helped his health and lifestyle.

Kate joins me on the Artichoke Series to discuss women's health issues. We will be working together in the new year to open the GSDF Women's Garden where it will be a safe place for women to talk about body image, women's health issues and so much more. Long term plans include women's retreats.

You can listen to their show online and find them on FaceBook. They interview some amazing world

healers. They also have a special gift for the GSDF Community.
http://www.extremehealthradio.com/gsdf

-------DR. ARINN TESTA, PSY D.

Dr. Arinn Testa is a dear friend and collaborator with GSDF. She comes on board to discuss stress and the emotional brain as well as ways to manage grief, health issues and loss. Dr. Testa helps teach us what the brain does in regards to our behaviors, our illness and how to create healthy change. Dr. Testa is the founder of Holistic Psychotherapy of Marin and is the Director of Clinical Training at EBT Connect. She always takes the time to answer questions from the GSDF Community when she is live. http://www.arinntesta.com/

-------SUSIE BACK

Susie Back is a dear friend and talented graphic design artist. She took the vision we had of GSDF and made our colors, logos and all of our book covers pop with life and color. She is always on the end of those notes: "I just finished my book, can you do the cover?" Where she asks when I need it by. My answer is usually today or tomorrow! http://www.backviewcreative.com/

-------CAROL NEU

Who constantly helps me, supports me and gives advice. She is always very willing to jump in and give me an extra hand whenever I need it. She helps support the GSDF Community in so many ways that most people do not even realize. I could not help as many people without the help and support that Carol gives not only to the community but to me. She helps me make my digital books look like real books and also does a lot of our graphics we use in groups, challenges and newsletters. http://neuworlddesigns.com/

-------BEANYE TROXELL AND GREG MROZINSKI

This lovely couple from Clear Lake City, Texas and have become a huge support to our GSDF Community. Beanye is one of our recipe testers and community leaders. Greg makes sure when his patients have to go GSDF that they find us so that we can help make the transition easier on them. They have inspired us to create lots of new cooking courses this year and support groups to help people. We are lucky to have them in our community.
visit our website:
http://glutensugardairyfree.com

Introduction

GSDF is short for Gluten, Sugar and Dairy Free. Whether you have food allergy, sensitivity or other medical condition, or you are giving up gluten, sugar and/or dairy by choice, it can be quite overwhelming knowing what is safe to eat, how to cook a different way and what to have on hand to make healthy meals.

I had to become gluten, sugar, dairy free for health reasons and at first it was a struggle. As I began to study with some of the top alternative care practitioners and began to learn how and what to eat for my health, I struggled to find recipes that were all three: gluten, sugar and dairy free. Most recipes were normally just free of one of the ingredients. So I began to re-write my cookbooks so that all of my new recipes were GSDF.

I discovered the health benefits of herbs, juicing and found healthy ways to recreate some of my favorite dishes. Along the way I have lost over 200 pounds and am still getting healthy. I started a website that grew into a huge community where I teach cooking classes, educational classes about being GSDF, budget friendly classes, holiday classes and more. We have an Artichoke Series that features guest experts teaching health and wellness with live Q&A.

This book is a collection of my poultry recipes. All the recipes are gluten, sugar and dairy free. The average prep time for the recipes are 15 minutes or less so that they are easy to do even if you are not well.

I pride myself on using normal, simple and fresh ingredients that can be found at most supermarkets. I do not use strange, expensive ingredients that you would only use once!

Michelle E. DeBerge.

Contents

CHICKEN IN THE SLOW COOKER 82

CHICKEN SOUPS 118

CHICKEN ON THE STOVETOP 136

ALL TURKEY 172

Organic Chicken

Let's discuss what an organic chicken really means. A lot of people go out their way to buy chicken that is labeled "organic" yet some chickens are also labeled free range, natural, cage free, antibiotic free, farm raised, and hormone free. What does it all really mean?

In order to be **certified as organic** by the government a chicken not only needs to be fed a completely vegetarian feed, this feed cannot have any GMO's or ever been treated with pesticides. The chicken can never be treated with hormones or antibiotics, except for medical reasons.

Cage free and free range. These terms are loosely used. Cage free means the chicken is not raised in a cage, but they do not have access to the outside and there are no specifics on how big the indoor facility needs to be.

Free range just means that the chickens are allowed outside, but again, there are no specifications to the size of the yard they are allowed out into.

GMO's. A chicken that is labeled no GMO means that the GMO ingredients in the feed is less than .09% and it needs to be verified before it can be labeled.

Natural means it's really chicken, nothing more.

No antibiotic means that the chicken was not treated by antibiotics before or after hatching. However, there is not verification process.

Easy Way to Shred Chicken

Having shredded chicken on hand makes meals quick. You can toss some in a salad, add to a sauce, wrap in a lettuce wrap with veggies, add to an omelet, add to a soup or just snack on. There are several ways to shred chicken quickly!

Use two forks and pull apart.

If you have boneless skinless chicken, use your hand mixture. The beater blades shred it very fast.

Pull it apart with your fingers.

Secret to Juicy Boneless Skinless Chicken Breast

I knew there had to be a secret to a juicy baked boneless skinless chicken breast. I had recently moved to a new state and struggled to find organic bone in skin on chicken breasts unless they were in a mega pack. In fact it seemed like I landed in the land of the boneless skinless chicken breast. I could find legs, thighs but no breasts with skin. Without the fat to protect the meat and the bone to impart flavor, my chicken breasts were rubbery disasters. I could marinade them so I would get flavorful rubbery breasts. It was driving me mad.

Most nights I work late and would rather toss my dinner in the oven to cook as I finish up my writing. I did not want to have to constantly sauté them. Sure I could cook them in the pressure cooker and then toss them in some sauce, but I wanted baked chicken. So I started doing some research. I tried many ways that folks wrote worked. Nothing did until two nights ago.

Two nights ago I made enough veggies for my side in case I had failure again. To my shock and joy, I had the most moist and tasty baked skinless boneless chicken breast ever. I did it again last night, yup it worked. I had my friends and VIP Foodie Testers try it today to make sure. They all reported back with surprise that it worked.

So are you ready for the secret?

Fill a bowl up with warm water and salt to make a brine. Then put your chicken breast in to that for 15 minutes while you heat up your oven to 450 degrees F. Take a casserole dish and pour a little olive oil in it. (Last night I used a lemon infused olive oil.) Rinse your chicken, pat it dry. Roll it all over in the olive oil so it coats all of the exterior of the chicken. Then sprinkle both sides with salt, pepper and herbs of your choice. (I used Herbs de Provence) Bake your chicken uncovered 15-18 minutes depending on the size of it. (Mine took 16 minutes both times) Take it out of the oven, cover with a foil tent and let it sit for 10 minutes. No peeking or rushing. (I think this is the magic step.) Then roll your chicken in the little bit of juices in the dish and serve. You will have a very juice tasty baked chicken breast.

The fun part is you can season it with whatever herbs you want and use different flavored olive oils for variety.

Finally I have my baked chicken again.

CHICKEN IN
THE OVEN

BAKED CHICKEN AND MUSHROOMS

The mushrooms, coconut milk, thyme, oregano and Dijon mustard create a delicious sauce for the tender chicken breasts. Simple to make and full of flavor.

SERVES: 4; PREP TIME:15 MINS; COOK TIME: 1 HOUR

Ingredients

- 4 bone in chicken breasts
- 3 cloves garlic minced
- 8 ounces baby bella mushrooms, cut in quarters
- ¼ yellow onion minced
- ¾ cup chickenstock
- 2 tbl coconut oil
- 1 tea thyme divided
- ½ tea oregano
- ½ cup coconut milk
- 1 tbl dijon mustard
- ½ teaspoon salt divided
- black pepper to taste

Directions

1. Pre-heat oven to 400 degrees

2. Season chicken breasts with salt, pepper and half of the thyme.

3. In large skillet heat the coconut oil over medium heat. Add the chicken skin side down and sear until golden brown about 4 minutes. Add the

garlic, onion and mushrooms. Cook until browned about 6-8 minutes. Add the salt, pepper, thyme, oregano and mustard. Stir well.

4. Add the stock and coconut milk and bring up to heat stirring well. Once up to a boil. Turn off heat and add the chicken breasts skin side up. Cook in oven until done about 35-40 minutes.

5. Remove chicken to platter and cook the mushroom mixture until liquid is reduced for about 5 minutes. Taste for salt and pepper. Pour over chicken and serve.

BASIL LEMON CHICKEN

This is one of my fresh, easy go to meals. This is perfect for the days when you come home from work hungry and tired. Slide this in the oven, put your feet up and enjoy the aroma as it bakes. It is almost like a pesto chicken but lighter. The freshness of the basil and lemon compliment the roast chicken.

SERVES: 4; PREP TIME:5 MINS; COOK TIME: 30 MINS

Ingredients

- 3 cups fresh basil leaves
- 5 tablespoons lemon juice
- 4-5 cloves garlic
- ¾ cup olive oil
- ¼ teaspoon salt
- 4 boneless, skinless chicken breast

Directions

1. Pre-heat the oven to 350 degrees F.
2. Place the first five ingredients into the blender and blend well.
3. In a small baking dish, place chicken breasts and pour sauce over.
4. Bake in a 350° oven for 30-40 minutes.

Serving Suggestions: The extra sauce is good as a salad dressing or over grilled fish. Add lemon zest for an extra punch. Sauce will stay fresh for 3 days in the refrigerator.

CHICKEN BELLA

Bella means beautiful and that is what this dish is. The creamy sauce made with cashew cream, garlic, white wine, turmeric, mushrooms, bell pepper and oregano coats the tender chicken breast pieces.

SERVES: 4-6; PREP TIME:20 MINS; COOK TIME: 45 MINS

Ingredients

- 4 boneless skinless chicken breasts cut into bite size pieces
- 2 cups chicken stock
- ½ cup cashew cream
- 1 red bell pepper cut into bite size pieces
- 8 ounces baby bella mushrooms sliced
- ½ bunch baby asparagus cut into one inch pieces
- 1 small yellow onion sliced thin
- 2 cloves of garlic minced
- 2 tablespoons coconut oil divided
- ¼ cup white wine
- 1 tea turmeric
- ½ tea oregano
- ¼ tea salt
- fresh black pepper

Directions

1. Prep your veggies on one board and your chicken on another board. Pre-heat oven to 350 degrees.

2. In a large skillet over medium high heat, melt the coconut oil. Add the veggies and sauté until the onion is translucent. Put in a large bowl to cool when done. In the same skillet add the second tablespoon of coconut oil and heat over medium high heat. Add the chicken pieces and cook until cooked through. Add to the same bowl with the veggies.

3. In the same skillet over medium high heat, add the chicken stock, white wine, the cashew cream, turmeric, oregano, salt and fresh black pepper. Once it comes to heat lower and simmer for 5 minutes. Add to the chicken and veggie mixture.

4. Pour the mixture into a casserole dish. You may cover it and cook it the next day or bake for 45 minutes uncovered in 350 degree oven.

CHICKEN CACCIATORE

This is a super easy dish to make that has wonderful flavor and turns out great every time. Even if this is your first time to make Chicken Cacciatore and you have guests coming over for dinner, do it! The sauce is full of flavor with all of the veggies and herbs. The one trick to the dish is to brown the chicken well on all sides before putting it into the sauce.

SERVES: 4-6; PREP TIME: 15 MINS; COOK TIME: 45 MINS

Ingredients

- 1 chicken cut into pieces
- 2 teaspoons salt
- 1 teaspoon pepper
- 2 tablespoons coconut oil
- 1 red bell pepper sliced thin
- 1 yellow onion, sliced thin
- 8 ounces mushrooms sliced

- 4 cloves of garlic, minced
- ¾ cup white wine
- 1 can fire roasted tomatoes
- 1 cup chicken stock
- 3 tablespoons capers
- 1 teaspoon dried oregano
- 1 teaspoon dried basil
- handful fresh basil leaves, chopped

Directions

1. Preheat oven to 350 degrees F.

2. Sprinkle the chicken pieces with salt and pepper.

3. In a large deep oven proof skillet, melt the coconut oil.

4. Add the chicken and cook until golden brown, 5-6 minutes per side.

5. Put chicken on platter to sit.

6. Add the wine to the skillet and bring up to bubble. Then add the stock, capers, oregano, basil, tomatoes, garlic, onions, mushrooms and bell peppers. Cook for 10 minutes stirring well.

7. Add the chicken to the sauce, nestling the pieces into the sauce.

CHICKEN DIVAN CASSEROLE

This recipe is my version of the classic chicken divan that was so popular in the 1960's and 1970's. The original dish was made with cream of chicken soup, mayo, sour cream and cheddar cheese. I replaced all of those ingredients with cashew cream and coconut milk. Then I added more flavor with lemon juice, madras curry powder and good white wine. The cashew cream thickens the sauce as it bakes in the oven. The result is a very tasty dish that is similar to the original but dairy free and much more healthy.

SERVES: 4; PREP TIME: 20 MINS; COOK TIME: 60 MINS

Ingredients

- 2 large roasted chicken breasts
- 4 cups broccoli florets
- ½ coconut milk
- ½ cup cashew cream
- zest one lemon
- juice of one lemon
- ¼ white wine
- ¼ teaspoon black pepper
- ½ teaspoon salt
- 2 teaspoons madras curry powder
- sprinkle of salt and pepper

Directions

1. Preheat oven to 350

2. Steam the broccoli until it is just fork tender. Put on a platter. Sprinkle with salt and pepper. Let cool.

3. Dice the chicken breasts into cubes.

4. In a large bowl mix the coconut milk, cashew cream, lemon zest, lemon juice, white wine, black pepper, sea salt and madras curry powder.

5. Add the cooled broccoli and cubed chicken to the sauce. Stir gently until everything is coated in the sauce.

6. Pour into a small baking dish using your spatula to flatten out the top of the casserole.

7. Cover tightly with foil.

8. Bake for 30 minutes covered and another 30 minutes uncovered.

9. Let sit for 5 minutes so that the sauce can settle. Enjoy!

CHICKEN SHAWARMA

Lemon, garlic, cumin, paprika, turmeric and cinnamon take ordinary chicken and make it extraordinary! Chicken and cinnamon go so we'll together.

Ingredients

- 2 lemons, juiced
- ½ cup plus 1 tablespoon olive oil
- 9 cloves garlic, peeled, minced
- 1 teaspoon salt
- 2 teaspoons freshly ground black pepper
- 2 teaspoons ground cumin
- 2 teaspoons paprika
- ½ teaspoon turmeric
- ½ teaspoon ground cinnamon
- Pinch Red pepper flakes
- 2 pounds boneless, skinless chicken thighs or breasts
- 2 large red onions, peeled and quartered

Directions

1. Combine the lemon juice, 1/2 cup olive oil, garlic, salt, pepper, cumin, paprika, turmeric, cinnamon and red pepper flakes in a large bowl, then whisk to combine.

2. Add the chicken and toss well to coat.

3. Cover and store in refrigerator for at least 1 hour and up to 12 hours.

4. Use the remaining tablespoon of olive oil to grease a rimmed sheet pan.

5. Add the onion to the chicken and marinade, and mix well.

To cook in the oven:

1. Heat oven to 425 degrees.

2. Remove the chicken and onion from the marinade, and place on the pan, spreading everything evenly across it.

3. Put the chicken in the oven and roast until it is browned, crisp at the edges and cooked through, about 30 to 40 minutes until internal temp of 165 F.

4. Serve over mixed greens with cucumbers, tomatoes and fresh chopped parsley. Or in a lettuce wrap.

To Grill:

1. Heat the grill to medium high.

2. Put the chicken on skewers for easier cooking.

3. Put the onions on separate skewer and grill.

4. Grill 12-15 minutes until done, turning once.

CHICKEN VERDE

This recipe is so easy and tasty. The best part is that it presents well and the unexpected flavor will wow any dinner guest, even your boss! I am giving you two versions. The roasted one has a little more flavor but the boiled one is still super delicious. After I make it, I cool it down before pouring it over the raw chicken to bake. Super easy, super tasty!

SERVES: 4; PREP TIME: 15 MINS; COOK TIME: 65 MINS

Ingredients

- 15-20 tomatillos
- 2 cloves garlic
- ½ teaspoon salt
- 1 jalapeño
- 1 small bunch fresh cilantro
- 4 boneless skinless chicken breasts

Directions

1. Pre-heat oven to 400 degrees F.
2. Peel and wash the tomatillos.
3. Place the tomatillos and the jalapeño on a sheet pan.
4. Drizzle a little olive oil over the veggies. Bake a 20-30 minutes.

5. Place the roasted vegetables in the blender.

6. Add the cilantro and the garlic clove. Blend well. Add the salt.

7. Blend again until smooth.

8. Cool the sauce.

9. Put the chicken breasts in a casserole dish and pour the sauce over. Bake for 30-40 minutes until they are cooked through.

10. Serve chicken with sauce spooned over.

11. If you have leftovers, shred the chicken in the sauce, put in fridge. Next day, heat on stove top and serve in lettuce wraps with some sliced avocado.

So-So

CLASSIC ROAST CHICKEN BREASTS

Make sure you use a chicken breast that has the bone in, it adds a lot of flavor. I love the smell of garlic and rosemary in the air as it cooks. I also like to roast a few extra breasts for salads and sandwiches the next day. By cooking it this way, the breast soaks up a lot of flavor.

SERVES: 4; PREP TIME: 10 MINS; COOK TIME: 45 MINS

Ingredients

- 4 chicken breasts bone in
- 10 garlic cloves smashed
- ½ teaspoon black pepper
- 2 lemon juiced
- 2 sprig of fresh rosemary
- ½ teaspoon salt
- 2 tablespoons olive oil

Directions

1. Pre-heat oven to 350 degrees F.
2. Wash and dry chicken breasts leaving skin intact. Place in a plastic zip bag.
3. In a bowl mix the lemon juice, olive oil, smashed garlic cloves, rosemary, salt and pepper.

4. Pour over chicken breasts in plastic bag and seal. Refrigerate for 2 hours, turning the bag over once after 1 hour.

5. Remove chicken from marinade and place on a small cookie sheet or a small baking dish. Bake 350° for 45 minutes.

6. The chicken is done when the juices run clear or it reaches 165° internally.

COQ AU VIN

Coq au vin is a French dish that is made with chicken braised in red wine with mushrooms, bacon, carrots, onion and garlic. Julia Child made this dish on her PBS show The French Chef, in the 1960's often and it became popular in the United States.

SERVES: 4; PREP TIME: 15 MINS; COOK TIME: 1 HR 30 MINS

Ingredients

- 1 3-4 pound chicken, cut into pieces
- ½ pound carrots, cut into 1-inch pieces
- ½ pound cremini mushrooms, stems trimmed
- ½ pound frozen pearl onions, defrosted
- 1 cup chicken stock
- ½ bottle red wine, usually a Burgundy
- 4 cloves garlic, minced
- 1 yellow onion, sliced
- 4 slices of bacon, diced
- 2 tablespoons coconut oil
- 1 ½ teaspoons dried thyme
- ½ teaspoon salt
- fresh ground black pepper

Directions

1. Heat the oven to 350 F degrees.

2. In a large dutch oven over medium high heat melt the coconut oil. Add the bacon and cook until lightly browned, about 8 minutes. Remove from the oil, leaving the oil and fat in the pan.

3. Sprinkle the chicken pieces with salt and pepper on both sides and put into the pan in a single layer. Brown each side, about 5-8 minutes. Set on a platter and do the next batch of chicken until they are all done.

4. Then add the carrots, onions, salt, pepper and thyme to the pan, stirring over medium high heat for 10 minutes until the onions are brown. Add the garlic and cook 1 more minute.

5. Add the chicken to the pot and the juices off the platter. Add the onions, mushrooms, the wine and stock and bring to a simmer. Cover and bake in the oven for 75 minutes until the chicken is cooked.

CREAMY MUSHROOM CHICKEN

This is a very easy delicious dinner that is also perfect for company. It comes out fantastic every time! I love creamy mushroom sauce and chicken but I did not want to stand over the stove the entire time.

SERVES: 4; PREP TIME: 10 MINS; COOK TIME: 60 MINS

Ingredients

2
- 4 bone in chicken breasts
1½
- 3 cloves garlic, minced
4
- 8 ounces cremini mushrooms, halved
½
- ¾ cup chicken stock
.375
- ¾ teaspoon dried thyme

- ½ tea salt   ⅛
- ¼ tea black pepper   ⅛
- ½ cup coconut milk
- 1 tablespoon dijon mustard   ½

Directions

1. Preheat oven to 350 degrees F.
2. Season chicken breasts with a pinch of salt and pepper.
3. In a large bowl add the garlic, mushrooms, chicken stock, salt, pepper, coconut milk and

mustard. Mix well making sure that all the ingredients are incorporated.

4. Put the mushroom mixture on the bottom of a baking dish. Place the chicken breasts on top. Bake for one hour.

5. Pull the chicken out of the sauce, set aside and cover to keep warm.

6. Stir the mushroom sauce, if it is too thin, pour the mushroom mixture in a sauce pan and cook for about 5-10 minutes over medium heat until thickens more. ✸

7. Plate the chicken and pour the sauce over.

Veeygord

✸ thicken w/ GF Flour — before baking

✸ eliminate Salt — was pretty salty

If use chicken strips — cook 20min

EASY LEMON CHICKEN

In the 1960's it was fashionable to coat a chicken breast with mayo and sprinkle it with parmesan cheese for a quick "gourmet" dinner. This is the same idea. Now that we are eating more boneless/skinless chicken breasts this recipe works great. Adding the lemon juice and zest adds a huge flavor punch.

SERVES: 4; PREP TIME: 5 MINS; COOK TIME: 40 MINS

Ingredients

- 4 boneless, skinless, chicken breast
- 1 tablespoon coconut oil
- pinch of salt
- pinch of pepper
- ½ cup good mayo
- 1 lemon

Directions

1. Preheat oven to 350 degrees
2. Coat the inside of a baking dish with the coconut oil
3. Sprinkle salt and pepper over both sides of the chicken breasts lightly. Place chicken breasts into baking dish

4. Mix the juice of the lemon and the lemon zest from the lemon and the mayo. Using a spoon coat each breast of chicken with the mayo mixture

5. Bake uncovered 35-40 minutes until juices run clear.

GARLIC LEMON CHICKEN THIGHS

This lemon, rosemary garlic baked chicken thighs over sliced onions is a perfect one pot dish. You could add sliced potatoes if you wanted. This recipe is using thighs but it could be used with legs, bone in breasts or the whole chicken. I you cook the chicken whole and not cut up increase the cooking time.

SERVES: 4; PREP TIME:15 MINS; COOK TIME: 50 – 60 MINS

Ingredients

- 8 chicken thighs
- 2 large yellow onions
- 2 lemons
- 1 head of garlic
- 2 sprigs fresh rosemary, or 1 tablespoon dried
- 1 ½ teaspoons salt
- ½ teaspoon fresh black pepper

Directions

1. Zest and juice one lemon and put into a large zip bag.

2. Mince 6 cloves of garlic and add to the bag.

3. Take the rosemary leaves off the stalk and corse chop, add to the bag.

4. Add the salt, pepper and chicken thighs and shake it well to get the marinade all over the chicken. Then take out the excess air and let marinate in fridge for 4 hours to over night.

5. Heat oven to 400 degrees farenheight

6. Slice onions into thick rings and place on the bottom of baking dish.

7. Remove the chicken from the marinade and place on top of the onions skin side up.

8. Slice the last lemon into rings and lay over the top of the thighs. This is for flavor, discard them before serving the chicken.

9. Bake uncovered 50-60 minutes until done.

LEMON TARRAGON CHICKEN

SERVES: 4; PREP TIME:15 MINS; COOK TIME: 60 MINS

Ingredients

- 4 skinless bone-in chicken breasts
- 2 tablespoons olive oil
- 4 tablespoons tarragon leaves
- ½ Tsp. salt
- ¼ Tsp. ground pepper
- 2 onions, peeled, halved and sliced into half rings
- 2 cups gluten-free low-sodium chicken broth
- 2 lemons, juiced

Directions

1. Preheat oven to 350°F
2. Toss chicken pieces with olive oil and half the tarragon leaves.
3. Season liberally with salt and pepper and toss well to make sure all pieces are evenly coated.
4. Arrange onion slices in the bottom of a baking pan or oven-proof Dutch oven large enough to hold chicken pieces as best as possible in one layer.
5. Sprinkle remaining half of tarragon leaves over onions and arrange chicken on top.

6. Add chicken broth and lemon juice, cover place in the oven.

7. Bake for about an hour or until juices run clear when chicken pieces are pierced with a fork.

8. Remove from oven, covered, and let rest 10 minutes.

9. Just before serving, taste the juices at the bottom of the pan and adjust seasoning with salt and pepper.

10. Serve chicken with juices spooned over it.

MAPLE DIJON CHICKEN

I wanted to create a chicken dish that was a little different, easy to do and came out perfect every time. I started thinking of flavors and came across my maple syrup that my friend from Canada had brought me. The dish turned out perfectly and it has become one of my more popular dishes with my readers.

SERVES: 4; PREP TIME: 15 MINS; COOK TIME: 60 MINS

Ingredients

- 4 bone in skinless chicken breast
- ¼ cup dijon mustard
- 3 Tbs maple syrup
- 1 Tbs oil
- pinch of red pepper flakes
- ½ tsp pepper
- ½ tsp salt
- zest of ½ lime
- 2 Tbs + extra for garnish chopped parsley
- 1 large clove of garlic
- 1 Tbs coconut oil or vegetable oil

Directions

1. Preheat oven to 350 degrees fahrenheit
2. Combine Dijon mustard, garlic clove, parsley, maple syrup, red pepper flakes, salt, black pepper and lime zest into a blender and blend

well, scraping sides periodically until it is all incorporated.

3. Remove 2 Tablespoons of the mixture and save for later in a small bowl.

4. Pour the remaining marinade into large plastic zip bag and add the chicken breasts.

5. Marinate in the refrigerator over night, at least a for a minimum of four hours for best results.

6. Rub the inside of a large baking dish with the oil.Pour the contents of the zip bag into a large baking dish and arrange the chicken breasts bone side down. Bake for one hour.

7. Use reserved 2 Tbs of marinade to baste chicken during the last 15 minutes.

8. While chicken is baking, chop a little fresh parsley to use as garnish.

9. Broil for 5 min to brown after it bakes for the hour if needed.

10. Remove from oven, pour any extra sauce over the breasts and garnish with a little chopped parsley.

MOROCCAN INSPIRED CHICKEN

I usually make a big batch of the rub up because I use it so often! The flavors of cumin, allspice, cinnamon, chili powder and hot madras curry powder is fantastic.

SERVES: 4; PREP TIME: 15 MINS; COOK TIME: 50 MINS

Ingredients

- 1 tablespoon dried cumin
- 1 tablespoon chili powder
- $1\,^{1}/_{12}$ teaspoons allspice
- $1\,^{1}/_{12}$ teaspoons black pepper
- $1\,^{1}/_{12}$ teaspoons cinnamon
- 1 teaspoon ancho chili powder
- $1\,^{1}/_{12}$ teaspoons hot madras curry powder
- 1 whole chicken
- 4 tablespoons olive oil

Directions

1. Mix all the rub ingredients in a container with a tight lid and shake.

2. Coat the chicken with the oil and then sprinkle the rub on it. Making sure the rub gets all over the exterior of the chicken.

3. Put back in fridge uncovered for 1-3 hours.

4. Then bring up to room temp, sprinkle a little more rub on the chicken and bake 400 degrees F.

5. Cook 1 - 1 ½ hours or until the chicken reaches 165 degrees.

6. Pull out of the oven and let set 15 minutes for the juices to redistribute.

7. Carve and serve.

ORANGE ROAST CHICKEN BREASTS

These orange roast chicken breasts are delicious! The zest and juice of fresh oranges, honey, rosemary and a touch of spice make them really become the star of the plate. The honey also caramelizes while cooking so the skin gets really nice and crispy.

SERVES: 4; PREP TIME: 10 MINS; COOK TIME: 60 MINS

Ingredients

- 4 chicken breasts or one chicken divided
- 5 tablespoons honey
- zest of 2 oranges
- juice of 2 oranges
- 6 tablespoons rosemary leaves chopped
- 1 tablespoon salt
- 2 teaspoons red pepper flakes
- ¾ teaspoon freshly ground black pepper

Directions

1. Pre-heat oven to 350 degrees F.

2. In a large bowl, mix together honey, orange juice, orange zest, rosemary, salt, red pepper flakes, and freshly ground black pepper. Add chicken pieces and turn to coat well.

3. Marinate 1 hour or up to over night.

4. Pull chicken out of marinade and put into a baking dish or on a sheet tray and bake for 50 minutes to one hour until done.

PECAN CRUSTED CHICKEN

Pecan crusted chicken was made in my kitchen when I had a hankering for fried chicken. I don't fry and I did not have any gluten free flour but I wanted juicy moist chicken with a crunch. I happened to have pecans on hand but you could use walnuts or almonds. I added lemon zest to balance the flavors of the nuts and a touch of cayenne chili for a bit of heat. That way the bite of moist chicken would be salty, sweet and spicy.

SERVES: 4; PREP TIME: 10 MINS; COOK TIME: 15 MINS

Ingredients

- 4 boneless skinless chicken breasts
- ½ cup pecans, chopped
- 2 teaspoons lemon zest
- ½ teaspoon salt
- ⅛ teaspoon cayenne chili
- a few grinds of fresh black pepper
- 1 egg, beaten
- 2 tablespoons water

Directions

1. Pre heat oven to 450 F

2. In a shallow bowl beat the egg and water.

3. In a food processor add the nuts, lemon zest, salt, pepper and chili. Pulse until the nuts are coarse like bread crumbs. Place on a plate.

4. Rinse and dry the chicken breasts. Put them into the egg mixture and coat all sides of the chicken.

5. Then put into the nut mixture and coat all sides.

6. Place in a casserole dish and pat any left over nut mixture on top of the breasts.

7. Bake for 15-18 minutes until the chicken reaches 165 degrees F.

8. Pull out of the oven, make a foil tent and let rest 10 minutes and then serve.

ROAST GARLIC CHICKEN

This roast garlic chicken was created one day when I was craving the 40 clove chicken from a restaurant in San Francisco called the Stinky Rose. They specialize in dishes with garlic. Their 40 clove chicken is divine. So this is my version of that dish. The chicken comes out moist, with crispy skin and flavored by not only the garlic but the fresh herbs.

Ingredients

- 1 whole chicken cut into pieces
- ½ Tsp. salt
- ¼ Tsp. black pepper
- 3 Tbsp. coconut oil
- 3 sprigs of parsley
- 5 sprigs of thyme
- 1 sprig of rosemary
- 1 whole head of garlic peeled
- ½ cup good white wine (stock can be substituted)

Directions

1. Heat oven to 350 degrees.
2. In large frying pan heat coconut oil.
3. Rinse chicken under cold water and dry .
4. Sprinkle chicken pieces with salt and pepper.
5. Place in frying pan to brown on each side taking care not to crowd the pan about 10 minutes

6. Tie herbs together with kitchen string (note if you don't have fresh herbs see note below recipe)*

7. In the bottom of a baking dish place the garlic cloves and the herbs.

8. Place chicken pieces on top of garlic, skin side up do not cover

9. Bake in oven 1 hour 20 minutes (until juices run clear)

10. Baste the chicken twice for best flavor

11. When done put chicken on plate to rest

12. Pour sauce and garlic cloves over chicken pieces

*Note: If you don't have fresh herbs, even though they are best in this recipe do this: ¼ tea thyme ¼ tea rosemary Mix the dried herbs and sprinkle over chicken pieces before baking.

SPICY CHICKEN LEGS

Sometimes you just need some nice spicy chicken legs for dinner, then this is the recipe for you! This recipe calls for the use of a grill pan and the oven so that you get a great char on the legs before they finish baking. You can also just grill the legs on the outside BBQ. This is a great dish to make for football Sunday's in front of the game instead of chicken wings. Though this marinade is great also on chicken wings.

SERVES: 4; PREP TIME: 10 MINS; COOK TIME: 20 MINS

Ingredients

- 4 whole skin on chicken legs
- ¼ cup rice vinegar
- 2 oranges
- 2 tablespoons Sriracha
- 3 cloves of garlic, minced
- 2 tablespoons tamari or coconut aminos
- 2 tablespoons organic raw honey
- 1 teaspoon red pepper flakes
- 2 tablespoons olive oil
- 1 tablespoon coconut oil
- ½ teaspoon salt
- fresh black pepper

Directions

1. Pre Heat oven to 400 degrees F.

2. Zest and juice one of the oranges, cut the other orange into 4 wedges.

3. In a large bowl, whisk together the rice vinegar, orange juice, orange zest, Sriracha, garlic, coconut aminos, honey, red pepper flakes, olive oil, salt and pepper.

4. Add the chicken legs and marinate for 30 minutes to two hours. I usually turn the legs over half way through or pour it all in a large zip bag.

Note: If you marinate the chicken over night, let it come up to room temperature before cooking because the honey gets a little hard in the fridge.

5. Heat a grill pan over medium heat and brush with a little coconut oil.

6. Remove the chicken from the marinade and place on the grill pan.

7. Cook each side 4-5 minutes each so that it gets a nice char.

8. Place pan into oven and bake for 10-15 minutes. The internal temperature of the chicken should be 165 degrees F.

9. Serve the chicken legs with a squeeze of the orange wedge over it.

STUFFED SWEET POTATOES

One day I was very tired and did not want to stand in the kitchen and cook. I wanted a one dish meal I could toss together with what I had on hand with ease. The final dish was a sweet potato stuffed with spinach, ground chicken and bell pepper. It was the perfect size and so tasty!

SERVES: 4; PREP TIME: 15 MINS; COOK TIME: 60 MINS

Ingredients

- 4 Sweet potatoes
- 1 pound ground chicken
- 2 cups baby spinach
- 1 red bell pepper, diced
- 1 yellow onion, diced
- 4 cloves of garlic, minced
- 1 teaspoon cumin
- 1 teaspoon cinnamon
- ½ teaspoon chili powder
- ½ teaspoon salt
- ¼ teaspoon pepper

Directions

1. Pre-heat oven to 425 degrees F.
2. Wash and dry potatoes. Pierce with a fork, put on a parchment sheet on a baking tray. Bake for one hour. Remove from oven and let cool a bit.

3. In a large skillet brown the ground chicken with the garlic and onions, about 5 minutes.

4. Add the bell pepper, the spices and the spinach to the chicken mixture mixing well. Cook until peppers are tender about 5 min.

5. Take the sweet potatoes and cut open with an X. Take a fork and mash the insides well and make a well in the center.

6. Add some of the beef mixture to each potato.

TURKEY TACO ZUCCHINI BOATS

Flavors of taco fill the mixture that is baked into the zucchini boats!.Top with fresh cilantro and avocado for a true feast!

SERVES: 4; PREP TIME: 10 MINS; COOK TIME: 50 MINS

Ingredients

- 4 medium zucchinis, cut in half lengthwise
- 1 pound ground turkey
- 2 roma tomatoes, diced
- 1 garlic clove, minced
- ½ yellow onion, minced
- ½ red bell pepper, minced
- 1 teaspoon cumin
- 1 teaspoon chili powder
- ½ teaspoon dried oregano
- ½ teaspoon salt
- 4 oz can tomato sauce
- ¼ cup water
- 2 tablespoons coconut oil
- ½ bunch fresh cilantro, chopped

Directions

1. Pre heat oven to 350 F.

2. Using a spoon or sharp knife, remove the center out of the zucchini halves, leaving ¼-inch outside area. Chop up the insides and set aside.

3. In a large skillet over medium high heat, melt the coconut butter. Add the turkey, cumin, chili powder, oregano and salt. Using a spatula to stir and break up the big pieces until done, about 4-5 minutes.

4. Add the onion, tomatoes, zucchini, garlic and bell pepper. Stir and cook for 1-2 minutes. Add 4/4 of the the tomato sauce and ½ of water, stir and simmer on low 15 minutes.

5. In the bottom of the baking dish, add the 1 ounce of tomato sauce and 2 tablespoons of water. Sprinkle with salt and pepper.

6. Place the zucchini boats in a baking dish and fill with the turkey taco mixture, pressing firmly to fill. Cover with foil and bake 30 minutes or until zucchini is done.

THAI STYLED CHICKEN BREAST

Very good
chicken is dry

SERVES: 4; PREP TIME: 10 MINS; COOK TIME: 60 MINS

1/3 *20 mN if*
cut breasts
in 1/2

Ingredients

- 4 chicken breasts bone in skin on   */*
- 3 chopped ginger   */*   *5 thin slices*
- 2 tablespoons chopped cilantro   *3/4*

- 3 garlic cloves chopped
- 2 stalks lemon grass   *3/4*
- 3 tablespoons tamari or coconut aminos   */*
- 1 lime juiced   *1 tablespoon*

Directions

1. Preheat oven to 350 degrees
2. Mix all ingredients in large zip bag. Add the chicken breasts.
3. Marinate 2-6 hours in the fridge. You can do this in the morning and bake in the evening.
4. Put chicken skin side up in a baking dish.
5. Bake chicken for one hour.

CHICKEN KABOBS AND SKEWERS

CHICKEN KABOBS

I love making chicken kabobs! It is a quick easy way to have dinner on the table quickly and it is a lot of fun. The best advice I can give you whenever you are making any type of kabobs; chicken, steak, shrimp or fish, is to do the protein on their own skewers and the veggies on their own. I know it looks pretty to have the veggies sprinkled among the protein pieces but veggies and the proteins have different cooking times.

You can marinade the veggies in the same marinade as the protein or you can follow my Roasted Balsamic Veggie recipe. Either way, make sure to separate the protein and the veggies. I always make double batches of the roasted veggies because they are great as a side dish the following night!

There are so many different marinades that you can put on grilled chicken kabobs. In fact you could make a different flavored chicken kabob every night of the week!

I personally generally use metal skewers but if you are going to use bamboo skewers, soak them in water for 1 hour before grilling to protect them from burning on the grill.

SERVES: 4 - 6; PREP TIME: 10 MINS; COOK TIME: 8 - 10 MINS

Ingredients

- 2 pounds boneless, skinless chicken breasts
- 2 lemons, juiced
- 1 orange, juiced
- 1 lime, juiced
- 4 garlic cloves, minced
- ⅓ cup tamari, coconut amino or gluten free soy sauce
- 2 teaspoons honey (may omit if sensitive)

Directions

1. In a large bowl mix all the ingredients except for the chicken with a whisk until well incorporated. Set aside.

2. Cut the chicken breasts into large size cubes.

3. Add the chicken to the bowl of marinade and mix well. Cover with plastic wrap or put in large zip bag and put into the fridge.

4. Let the chicken marinate for 3 hours or overnight.

Note: If using same marinade for veggies, separate some in a separate bowl to marinate separately. Do not put raw chicken and veggies together.

5. Pre heat your grill to 375 degrees (a medium hot fire).

6. Skewer the chicken pieces allowing them to lightly touch but not compacting them tightly together.

7. Cook chicken until tender and cooked through, 8-10 minutes turning to make sure all sides are cooked.

Note: To cook skewers in oven: Heat to 425 F. Arrange skewers on baking sheet in single layer and cook 10-12 minutes.

HONEY CHICKEN KABOBS

The honey adds a touch of sweet to the kabob but also helps the outside of the chicken pieces caramelize and become delicious. A pinch of red chili flakes adds to the flavor!

SERVES: 4; PREP TIME: 15 MINS; COOK TIME: 15 MINS

Ingredients

- 4 boneless skinless chicken breasts, cubed
- ⅓ cup honey
- ⅓ cup tamarin or coconut aminos
- 3 cloves garlic, minced
- ¼ teaspoon black pepper
- ½ teaspoon red chili flakes
- 4 green onions cut into 1-inch pieces
- 1 purple onion, cut into 1-inch pieces
- 1 red bell pepper, cut into 1-inch pieces
- 16 small mushrooms
- 2 tablespoons coconut oil

Directions

1. In a zip bag add the honey, tamari, garlic, black pepper, red chili flakes and green onion. Seal and shake to mix well. Add the cubed chicken, seal and shake to mix well. Put into the fridge for 2 hours or overnight.

2. Put the veggies on their own skewers and the chicken on their own.

3. Heat your grill to medium high heat and brush with the coconut oil. Put the skewers on the grill and cook for 12-15 minutes turning mid way through.

4. Take off the skewers and toss the chicken with the veggies.

MEDITERRANEAN CHICKEN KABOBS

The flavors of rosemary, oregano and fresh lemon juice whisk you away to the Mediterranean. These delicious kabobs have so much flavor they are great over a salad the next day!

SERVES: 6; PREP TIME: 15 MINS; COOK TIME: 8 - 10 MINS

Ingredients

- 1 ½ pounds boneless, skinless chicken breasts, cut into 1-inch pieces
- 4 cloves of garlic, minced
- 2 tablespoons fresh rosemary, chopped
- 1 teaspoon dried oregano
- ½ teaspoon salt
- ½ teaspoon pepper
- ⅓ cup fresh lemon juice
- zest of a lemon
- 2 tablespoons olive oil
- 1 red bell pepper, cut into 1-inch pieces
- 1 purple onion, cut into 1-inch pieces

Directions

1. In a large zip bag add the garlic, rosemary, oregano, salt, pepper, lemon juice, lemon zest and olive oil. Seal and shake to mix, Add the

chicken, seal and shake to mix. Marinade in fridge 2 hours.

2. Skewer the chicken, bell pepper and onion alternating for flavor.

3. Heat grill to medium high heat and put kabobs on, turning once cook 8 to 10 minutes until chicken is fully cooked.

MIDDLE EASTERN CHICKEN KABOBS

The mix of cardamon, cinnamon and oregano is the middle eastern flavor. I toss the cubed chicken in the herbs and let sit for 30 minutes to infuse the meat with flavor. This is a great way to have a healthy but tasty meal quickly.

SERVES: 4; PREP TIME: 15 MINS; COOK TIME: 15 MINS

Ingredients

- 1 pound chicken breasts cubed
- ½ yellow onion finely diced
- 2 minced cloves garlic
- 1 bell pepper
- 1 purple onion
- 8 mushrooms
- 1 tea oregano
- 1 tea cinnamon
- 1 tea cardamon
- ½ tea salt
- ¼ tea black pepper

Directions

1. In a large bowl mix the chicken, yellow onion, garlic, oregano, cinnamon, cardamom, salt and black pepper. Let sit for 30 minutes.

2. Cut the bell pepper and onion into pieces. Slice the mushrooms in half.

3. On skewers put some of the veggies then the meat, then veggies and then meat. Do this for 4 skewers.

4. Over medium high heat, grill the skewers for 5-6 minutes on each side until cooked. You can also cook the skewers under the broiler.

PINEAPPLE CHICKEN KABOBS

I love bell peppers, chicken and pineapple grilled together! this recipe has a hint of heat with the jalepenos in the marinade. The mix of pineapple, soy, honey, sesame oil, ginger and garlic will guarantee you the best tasting kabobs on the block.

SERVES: 4; PREP TIME: 15 MINS; COOK TIME: 15 MINS

Ingredients

- 1 pound boneless skinless chicken breasts, cubed
- 1 red bell pepper, cut into 1-inch chunks
- 1 yellow or orange bell pepper, cut into 1-inch chunks
- I purple onion, cut into 1-inch chunks
- 1 pineapple, cut into chunks
- ⅓ fresh pineapple juice
- 2 tablespoons coconut aminos or tamari
- 2 tablespoons honey
- 2 tablespoons rice vinegar
- 1 teaspoon sesame oil
- 2-inch piece of fresh ginger, grated
- 2 garlic cloves, minced
- 2 jalapeños, seeded and chopped

Directions

1. In a large zip bag add the pineapple juice, tamari, honey, rice vinegar, sesame oil, ginger, garlic and jalapeños. Seal and shake to mix. Add the chicken to the bag, seal, shake to mix and marinate for 3 hours.

2. Put the veggies, fruit and chicken onto skewers alternating.

3. Heat grill to medium high heat and cook skewers, turning once half way through 12-14 minutes.

THAI CHICKEN SKEWERS

These Thai Chicken Skewers have so much flavor that you can eat them as is but they are also very good dipped into the Thai Inspired Almond Nut Sauce.

SERVES: 10; PREP TIME: 10 MINS; COOK TIME: 5 - 7 MINS

Ingredients

- 2 pounds of chicken breast cut into strips (or use chicken tender pieces)
- ½ cup coconut aminos
- 4 tablespoons fresh lime juice
- 4 teaspoons fresh grated ginger
- $1\,^1/_{12}$ teaspoons red chili flakes
- 8-10 green onions chopped into 1 inch pieces (using the white and green parts)
- 1 teaspoon gram marsala curry powder

Directions

1. Mix all the ingredients except the chicken in a large plastic zip bag. If you want a little more marinade add a little water.

2. Once mixed, add the chicken strips and place in fridge. Marinate 4 hours to overnight. This allows the flavor to go deep into the chicken.

3. **BBQ:** Place the strips on a well heated BBQ, turning once. Takes about 3-4 minutes per strip. Make sure you cook the chicken all the way through.

4. **STOVE TOP:** Heat a non-stick frying pan over medium heat and cook the strips turning once.

CHICKEN SALADS

CHINESE CHICKEN SALAD

My Chinese Chicken Salad was created from a flavor memory of my favorite Chinese Chicken Salad from a restaurant in San Anselmo, located Northern California, called Comfort's. Comfort's was famous for their salads that were served in large Chinese take out boxes. The salad was put in first, then the chicken was laid on top, sprinkled with toasted almonds and sesame seeds. The dressing was nestled in a container in the side and a slice of orange laid on top. It was the perfect balance of flavors.

I add that touch of orange flavor to the my dressing and marinade along with sesame oil, fresh ginger and tamari. I mix shredded Napa cabbage and romaine lettuce for crunch and texture. Grated carrots, cilantro and green onions add flavor while the toasted sesame seeds and almonds add crunch. I usually make a double batch and keep the dressing separate so it lasts longer.

When I was in my 20's I had a seasonal restaurant at a private swim and tennis club in Ross, California. I began with mostly food for the kids in the summer camps but soon became a lunch place for the ladies. Comfort's had just opened and I loved their Chinese Chicken Salads and they allowed me to carry them at my place. Soon my little seasonal restaurant became very popular for lunch. I rounded out my menu with fresh veggie tostadas, veggie/shrimp rice paper rolls, other salads and soups. Yet I always sold out of the Comfort's Chinese Chicken Salad. People began to call and order theirs ahead.

Still today, Comfort's is a very busy place to find great food and a huge variety of healthy options. Yet their Chinese Chicken Salad is still a best seller! This is my version of their well loved salad.

SERVES: 4; PREP TIME: 15 MINS; COOK TIME: 10 MINS

DRESSING AND MARINADE

Ingredients

- ¼ cup Tamari or Coconut Aminos
- ¼ cup apple cider vinegar
- 1 Tablespoon olive oil
- 1 Tablespoon sesame oil
- 1 orange, juiced
- 3 Tablespoons fresh ginger, grated
- 3 green onions, chopped, white and green parts
- 1 tablespoon honey

SALAD

Ingredients

- 2 boneless skinless chicken breasts
- ½ Napa cabbage, cut into strips
- 1 romaine lettuce, cut into strips
- 3 carrots, grated or spiralized
- ½ cup slivered almonds, toasted
- ½ head of cilantro, chopped
- 3 green onions, green and white parts
- 1 teaspoon white sesame seeds, toasted
- 1 teaspoon black sesame seeds (or an additional 1 teaspoon toasted white sesame seeds)

Directions

For the marinade:

1. In a jar with a tight lid add tamari, ginger, olive oil, sesame oil, orange juice and the honey and shake well.

2. In a large zip bag, pour ¼ of the marinade, add the chopped onions and the chicken breasts and marinade for two hours or overnight. Put the jar of dressing in the fridge to get cold.

3. Either grill the chicken or cook in a grill pan on the stove over medium high heat. Cook 5 minutes on each side or until done and 165 degrees. Put on a plate and let it rest for 10 minutes so that the juices redistribute. Then cut the chicken into pieces or strips.

4. Shake the dressing well to make sure it is incorporated well. Then in a large bowl toss together cabbage, chicken, carrots, almonds, green onions, and cilantro with enough dressing to coat salad. Add the chicken on top and sprinkle with sesame seeds

CURRY CHICKEN SALAD

Curry chicken salad is one of my favorite dishes to have on hand for quick lunches. I normally make it with apples and celery in it. It is also great with nuts (toasted almond slivers or cashews), raisins or died cherries.

I like to use a curry blend that is easy to find and it is called Madras Hot Curry Powder. I don't know why they call it hot because it is not spicy. The blend has fenugreek, coriander, cumin, turmeric, red bell pepper and garlic in it.

SERVES: 4; PREP TIME: 15 MINS; COOK TIME: 40 - 50 MINS

Ingredients

- 3 bone in chicken breasts
- 1 ½ cups mayo
- 1 lemon juiced
- 3 tablespoons madras curry
- 2 stalks of celery, chopped
- 1 apple, peeled and diced
- ½ teaspoon black pepper
- salt and pepper
- ½ cup nuts, optional
- ¼ cups raisins or dried cherries, optional

Directions

1. Preheat oven to 350. Put the chicken breasts on a sheet pan and sprinkle with salt and pepper. Bake 40-50 minutes or until done.

2. Cool and then pull the meat from the bones and the skin off. Cut into bite size cubes and put into a bowl.

3. In a large bowl mix the dressing: add the mayo, lemon juice, curry powder and black pepper. Mix well and set aside.

4. Peel and core the apple, then dice into small chunks add to the bowl with the chicken.

5. Cut the celery in half length wise and then dice. Add to bowl with the chicken.

6. Add the nuts and dried fruit if desired to bowl also. Mix gently but make sure that all the ingredients are dispersed evenly.

7. Add the mix to the dressing and gently mix. Once mixed well refrigerate for at least an hour for the flavors to merge.

8. Serve on top of a mixed green salad.

GRAPE AND WALNUT CHICKEN SALAD

I love to have this chicken salad on hand for a quick lunch serving. It is a simple yet delicious recipe. Use a poached or roasted chicken breast. If you are in a hurry you can use the roast chicken from the grocery store.

SERVES: 4; PREP TIME: 15 MINS

Ingredients

- 4 chicken breasts poached or baked
- 2 cups grapes sliced in half
- 1 cup walnut pieces, toasted

- 2 tablespoon parsley minced
- ¾ cup good mayonnaise
- 3 grinds of fresh black pepper

Directions

1. Cut the cooked chicken into small pieces and put into a bowl.

2. In a pan with out any oil, toast walnuts to enhance their flavor. Make sure not to burn. Once cooled, chop into small pieces. Add to the bowl with the chicken.

3. Slices grapes in half and add to the bowl. Chop the parsley and add to the bowl.

4. In a bowl mix the chicken, grapes, walnuts, parsley, and the mayonnaise. Adding more mayonnaise as needed. Chill salad before serving.

GRILLED CHICKEN ASIAN SALAD

This grilled Chicken asian salad is the star of my table on hot summer nights. I love big bold flavors. This crunchy salad full of veggies and herbs is tossed in a bold and almost spicy dressing that pared with tender chicken, toasted sesame seeds and toasted almonds will have you going for seconds or licking your bowl.

SERVES: 10; PREP TIME: 10 MINS; COOK TIME: 20 MINS

Ingredients

- 4 boneless chicken breasts, grilled
- 1 napa cabbage, shredded
- 2 heads of romaine lettuce, shredded
- 2 carrots, grated
- 1 red bell pepper, thinly sliced
- ¼ cup slivered almonds, toasted
- 1 tablespoon toasted sesame seeds
- ¼ bunch of cilantro,
- ¼ bunch mint, leaves chopped
- ½ cup bean sprouts
- ¼ cup olive oil
- 2 tablespoons tamari or gluten free soy sauce
- 2 tablespoons rice vinegar
- 3 teaspoons fresh grated ginger
- 1 teaspoon sesame oil
- 1 teaspoon sriricha sauce

chopped

Directions

1. In large jar, add the olive oil, tamari, rice vinegar, ginger, sesame oil and sriracha shake well to incorporate it well.

2. Shred the napa cabbage and romaine lettuce and put in a large bowl.

3. Shred the chicken breasts with two forks or cut into cubes. Add to the bowl.

4. Add the grated carrot, bell pepper, almonds, sesame seeds, bean sprouts, cilantro and mint to the bowl.

5. Add the salad dressing and toss the salad well.

LEMON CHICKEN QUINOA WITH BEETS

I have found that adding distinct flavors and ingredients to quinoa, I have a quick healthy meal in a bowl in moments. I also love to put the quinoa over a simple salad of arugula with some oil and vinegar dressing it. This is a great source of protein and is delicious. The addition of the lemon juice at the end makes the quinoa fluffy and soft.

SERVES: 4; PREP TIME: 15 MINS; COOK TIME: 20 MINS

Ingredients

- 1 cup raw quinoa
- 2 cups water
- 1 lemon, juiced
- 1 cup roast chicken, shredded
- ½ cup spinach, cut into ribbons
- ½ orange bell pepper, diced
- 4 green onions, sliced
- 2 roasted red beets, peeled, cut into pieces.

Directions

1. In a pan put the quinoa and water in, bring to boil. Cover and simmer according to time directions.

2. When it is done, pour in the lemon juice, quickly stir with a fork and cover. Let it sit like that until it is cool.

3. In a large bowl add the rest of the ingredients and the quinoa, toss.

4. Serve as is or over salad.

ROAST CHICKEN SALAD WITH APPLE

This is a very easy recipe to make and can even be made with store bought rotisserie chicken in a pinch. The celery and and ap- ple add a nice crunch and the apple adds a great sweetness that pairs perfectly with the chicken.

SERVES: 4; PREP TIME: 15 MINS; COOK TIME: 45 MINS

Ingredients

- 2 breasts of chicken, bone in 1 apple
- 3 stalks of celery
- 1 lemon
- ¼ Tsp. salt
- ¼ Tsp. fresh black pepper
- 2 Tbsp. chopped parsley
- ½ cup mayo

Directions

1. Sprinkle some salt and pepper over the chicken breasts on both sides.

2. Cover a baking sheet with foil and pre-heat oven to 350 de- grees

3. Put chicken skin side up on cookie sheet and bake for 45 min- utes

4. Let chicken cool, cut off the bone and dice into bite size pieces.

5. Chop the apple and the celery into very small pieces.

6. In a large mixing bowl add the mayo, chopped parsley, lemon juice, lemon zest and black pepper together.

7. Add the celery, apple and chicken to the mayo mix and stir well.

8. Put in refrigerator for at least an hour to chill.

9. Serve over mixed greens.

CHICKEN IN THE SLOW COOKER

ARTICHOKE AND CHICKEN

I love the mix of artichokes, lemon, garlic and chicken. This slow cooker dish takes all of those flavors with the addition of mushrooms and cooks it to perfection. Serve as is or over rice to soak up the sauce. Quick cooking tapioca is an easy to use thickener that is available in most markets. It does not have flavor so it allows the bold tastes of the dish to stand on their own.

SERVES: 8; PREP TIME: 20 MINS; COOK TIME: 180 - 300 MINS

Ingredients

- 8 boneless, skinless chicken thighs
- ½ cup chicken stock
- 1 package frozen artichoke hearts
- 1 cup mushrooms, sliced
- 1 red pepper, diced
- 1 Yellow onion, sliced
- 10 cloves garlic, peeled
- 1 lemon, zested and juiced
- 1 tablespoon quick-cooking tapioca
- 2 teaspoons dried rosemary
- ½ teaspoon salt
- ½ teaspoon ground black pepper
- 2 tablespoons parsley, chopped

Directions

1. Place the artichokes, mushrooms, onions and garlic on the bottom of slow cooker.

2. Place the chicken on top of the veggies.

3. In a bowl mix the stock, lemon juice, lemon zest, quick cooking tapioca, rosemary, salt and pepper. Pour over the chicken.

4. Cover and cook on low for 5 hours or on high for 2/12 hours.

5. Stir well and serve garnished with diced red pepper and parsley.

CHICKEN AND RED POTATOES

SERVES: 4; PREP TIME: 10 MINS; COOK TIME: 4 HOURS

Ingredients

- 4 boneless skinless chicken breasts
- 8 small red potatoes, quartered
- 4 carrots, peeled and cut into ½ inch slices
- 18 oz container mushrooms, quartered
- 1 can fire roasted green chilies
- 1 cup chicken stock
- 2 teaspoons tapioca starch
- ½ teaspoon poultry seasoning
- ½ teaspoon salt
- fresh black pepper
- ½ teaspoon thyme

Directions

1. Place the veggies in the bottom of the cooker.
2. Sprinkle the breasts with salt and pepper and place on top of the veggies.
3. Mix the rest of the ingredients and pour over the chicken and veggies.
4. Cover and cook on low for 4 hours. (Check at 3 ½)
5. Serve the veggies and chicken with the sauce poured over.

CHICKEN AND ROOT VEGGIES

This is a great way to get an assortment of root veggies with your chicken. Loads of flavor with rosemary, thyme and lemon.

SERVES: 4 - 6; PREP TIME: 15 MINS; COOK TIME: 7 HRS LOW

Ingredients

- 4 boneless chicken breasts, cubed
- 2 carrots, peeled, cubed
- 1 parsnip, peeled, cubed
- 1 turnip, peeled cubed
- 2 sweet potatoes, peeled cubed
- 1 ¾ cups chicken stock
- 1 lemon, zested, juiced
- 1 tablespoon coconut oil
- 1 teaspoon rosemary
- 1 teaspoon thyme
- ½ teaspoon salt
- ¼ teaspoon nutmeg
- fresh black pepper

Directions

1. In a larges skillet heat up the coconut oil.

2. Sprinkle chicken with salt and pepper, add to the pan and brown the pieces. About 3 minutes.

3. In the slow cooker mix all the ingredients together including the browned chicken.

4. Cover and cook on low for 7 hours.

CHICKEN AND WILD RICE SOUP

Chicken and wild rice soup is one of my favorite soups when I am under the weather. Since I am not a fan of gluten free noodles in soups, I have begun to turn to putting rice or quinoa in soups. This soup uses wild rice which I love because it holds up well during the long cooking process.

SERVES: 6 - 8; PREP TIME: 15 MINS; COOK TIME: 8 HRS LOW

Ingredients

- 1 pound chicken breasts, skin off
- 1 cup wild rice, uncooked
- 6 cups chicken stock
- 2 carrots, peeled, diced
- 2 stalks celery, diced
- 1 small yellow onion, diced
- 3 cloves garlic, diced
- 2 teaspoons poultry seasoning
- ½ teaspoon salt
- fresh black pepper

Directions

1. Put all the ingredients into the slow cooker, mix well, cover and cook for 7 hours on low.

2. Remove the chicken and shred with forks, put back into slow cooker, stir, cover and cook for 30 more minutes.

CHICKEN CACCIATORE

I love chicken cacciatore! The dish is simple with chicken, bell peppers, onion, garlic and tomatoes. Making this in the slow cooker means that the chicken will be perfectly tender and can be shredded and added back into the sauce to soak up more flavor.

SERVES: 4; PREP TIME: 10 MINS; COOK TIME: 7 HRS LOW

Ingredients

- 1 ½ pounds chicken thighs, boneless, skinless
- 1 can (28 oz) fire roasted tomatoes
- 6 oz tomato paste
- 1 red bell pepper, thinly sliced
- 1 green bell pepper, thinly sliced
- 1 yellow onion, thinly sliced

- 4 garlic cloves, minced ½ cup good red wine
- 1 teaspoon dried oregano
- 1 teaspoon dried basil
- 1 teaspoon salt
- ½ teaspoon fresh ground pepper
- 1 bay leaf

Directions

1. Mix all the ingredients except for the chicken in the slow cooker, nestle the thighs into the sauce, cover, cook on low for 7 hours.

CHICKEN STEW WITH GREEN OLIVES AND ALMOND

This chicken stew has onion, garlic, cumin, paprika, turmeric, green olives, lemon zest and fire roasted tomatoes. It cooks into a tender juice flavorful dish that is topped with toasted almonds for a satisfying crunch and served over a nice bed of lemon quinoa for a perfect dinner.

SERVES: 4; PREP TIME: 10 MINS; COOK TIME: 4 HRS HIGH

Ingredients

- 1 (3-pound) quartered chicken, skinned
- 2 (14.5-ounce) cans fire roasted tomatoes, drained
- 1 ½ cups chicken stock, divided
- 1 yellow onion, sliced
- 3 cloves garlic, minced
- 1 teaspoon cumin
- 1 teaspoon paprika
- 1 teaspoon turmeric
- ¼ teaspoon salt
- ½ teaspoon freshly ground black pepper
- ½ cup pitted green olives
- 1 lemon, zested
- ¼ cup sliced almonds, toasted

Directions

1. Add all the ingredients except for the olives, lemon zest and almonds in the slow cooker. Cover and cook on high 3.5 hours. Then add the lemon zest and the olives, stir, cover cook 30 minutes.

2. Remove the chicken from the slow cooker and remove all the bones. Stir the tender chicken meat into the veggies, cover and keep warm until ready to serve. Then top with toasted almond slices.

CROCKPOT CHICKEN TACO CHILI

When I lived in New Mexico as a girl I use to love to ski and would go up the mountain any chance I could. I would come home to a big pot of beef chili and beans cooking on the stove after a long day of skiing. I loved how the house smelled and eagerly looked forward to a huge bowl of it. Now back then I would eat bowls of it!

This is my version of that chili using chicken and green chilies. I love green chilies and I order 20 pounds of them every year from Hatch New Mexico. I roast them and put them in the freezer. The canned ones work fine for this recipe.

Make sure to shred the chicken meat half an hour or more before serving and let it soak up all the flavors of the sauce during that time. You will want bowls of this chili.

SERVES: 4 - 6; PREP TIME: 10 MINS; COOK TIME: 6 HOURS

Ingredients

- 4 skinless boneless chicken breasts
- 1 onion, finely chopped
- 1 16-oz can kidney beans rinsed
- 1 can fire roasted green chili
- 2 cans fire roasted tomatoes

- 2 tbsp cumin
- 2 tbsp chili powder
- ½ tea oregano
- ½ tea salt
- ¼ tea pepper
- ¼ cup chopped fresh cilantro (garnish)
- ½ finely diced onion (garnish)

Directions

1. Combine beans, onion, green chilies, fire roasted tomatoes and the seasonings in to a crock pot. Stir well.

2. Place chicken breasts on top of mixture and cover.

3. Cook on low for 8-10 hours or on high for 4-5 hours.

4. Half hour before serving, remove chicken and shred using two forks.

5. Return chicken to slow cooker and mix into the veggie mix, cover and cook 30 more min.

6. Top with fresh cilantro and onions.

CURRIED CHICKEN THIGHS

I love chicken and red curry. This is a perfect dish for the slow cooker. The thighs come out fork tender infused with the curry flavor. I like to pour extra sauce over the meat once I pull it off the bone.

SERVES: 8; PREP TIME: 5 MINS; COOK TIME: 7 HRS LOW

Ingredients

- 3 pounds chicken thighs, skin removed
- 1 cup tomato sauce
- 4 tablespoons red curry paste
- ½ cup unsweetened coconut milk
- 2 tablespoons yellow onion, diced
- ½ teaspoon dried basil
- ½ teaspoon salt

Directions

1. Combine all the ingredients except the thighs, in a slow cooker mix well.

2. Add the thighs and stir to make sure they are evenly coated.

3. Cook with the lid on for 7 hours on low.

HONEY SESAME CHICKEN

I was asked to create a GSDF recipe for Honey Sesame Chicken. If you are going to use honey, make sure to use a local raw organic honey. I make my own ketchup because then I know it does not have sugar in it. The recipe for that follows the main recipe.

SERVES: 4 - 6; PREP TIME: 10 MINS; COOK TIME: 4 HRS

Ingredients

- 2 pounds chicken thighs, boneless skinless
- 1 yellow onion, diced
- 4 cloves garlic, minced
- ½ cup honey
- ½ cup gf soy sauce or tamari or coconut amino
- ¼ cup ketchup - recipe follows
- ½ teaspoon sesame oil
- ½ teaspoon crushed red peppers
- 2 green onions, sliced for garnish
- 2 tablespoons sesame seeds, roasted for garnish

Directions

1. Put all the ingredients except the green onions, sesame seeds and chicken into a large bowl and mix well. Add the chicken and toss to coat.

2. Pour into slow cooker and cover. Cook 4 hours on low.

3. Remove the chicken and shred, add back to sauce.

4. Serve with green onions and sesame seeds.

KETCHUP RECIPE

Ingredients

- 1 can tomato paste
- 2 tablespoons apple cider vinegar
- ⅓ cup water
- ¼ teaspoon dry mustard
- ¼ teaspoon cinnamon
- ¼ teaspoon salt
- ¼ teaspoon onion powder
- ¼ teaspoon garlic powder
- ⅛ teaspoon cayenne pepper
- ⅛ teaspoon all spice

Directions

1. Whisk all ingredients together and put in fridge overnight.

ITALIAN STYLE CHICKEN BREASTS

This is an easy tasty one pot meal. Add a nice green side salad and dinner is done. The mix of Italian herbs, creamy beans and fire roasted tomatoes makes a great accompaniment to the moist tender chicken.

SERVES: 4; PREP TIME: 8 MINS; COOK TIME: 8 HRS

Ingredients

- 4 bone in chicken breasts, skin removed
- 1 can cannelloni beans, rinsed
- 1 can fire roasted tomatoes
- 3 cloves garlic, diced
- ½ yellow onion, diced
- 2 teaspoons basil
- 1 teaspoon oregano
- ½ teaspoon dreid red pepper flakes
- ½ teaspoon salt
- black pepper

Directions

1. Put the chicken breasts into the bottom of the slow cooker, bone side down.

2. Mix all the rest of the ingredients into a bowl and then pour over the chicken breasts.

3. Cover and cook 8 hours on low.

MEDITERRANEAN INFLUENCED CHICKEN

The flavors from lemons, olives and capers makes me think of the dishes that are regional to the Mediterranean. This is a very simple easy dish with great flavor. It is good enough to make for company. I normally serve this with either an herb rice or some garlic mashed potatoes and sautéed greens.

SERVES: 6; PREP TIME: 10 MINS; COOK TIME: 4 HRS LOW

Ingredients

- 3 large bone in chicken breasts, skinned, cut in half Or
- 12 bone in chicken thighs, skinned
- 1 can fire roasted tomaotes
- 1 lemon
- 1 yellow onion, diced
- 3 cloves garlic, minced
- ½ cup pitted kalamata olives
- 3 tablespoons capers
- ½ teaspoon thyme
- 1 bay leaf
- ½ teaspoon salt
- black pepper

Directions

1. Zest and juice the lemon and put into a bowl. Add the rest of the ingredients except the chicken and mix well.

2. Place the chicken in the bottom of the slow cooker and pour the sauce over.

3. Cover and cook on low 4 hours.

ORANGE GLAZED CHICKEN

The flavors of orange and balsamic really make these chicken thighs special. The ingredients not only infuse the chicken with flavor but create a fantastic sauce.

SERVES: 4 - 6; PREP TIME: 10 MINS; COOK TIME: 6 HRS LOW

Ingredients

- 6 chicken thighs
- 1 tablespoon coconut oil
- 1 orange, zested, juiced
- 2 yellow onions, sliced
- 1 cup veggie stock
- 2 teaspoons tapioca starch
- 2 tablespoons balsamic vinegar
- 1 tablespoon honey
- 1 teaspoon coconut aminos or tamari
- 1 clove garlic, minced
- ½ teaspoon cumin
- ¼ teaspoon salt
- fresh ground black pepper

Directions

1. In a large skillet add the coconut oil and coat the bottom of the pan.

2. Salt and pepper the thighs and then put in the skillet to brown both sides, about 3 minutes a side.

3. In a large bowl mix all the ingredients well.

4. Add the thighs and make sure they get evenly coated.

5. Pour into your slow cooker, cover and cook on low for 6 hours.

ROTISSERIE CHICKEN

Imagine coming home to the smell of roast chicken coming from your slow cooker where the meat is ready to fall off the bone. You gently lift it out and put it on a sheet tray under the broiler for a few minutes to crisp up the skin. When you bite into it you can taste in the infusion of all of the herbs cooked into the meat.

SERVES: 4 - 6; PREP TIME: 10 MINS; COOK TIME: 6-7 HOURS LOW 4-4.5 HOURS HIGH

Ingredients

- 1 whole roasting chicken
- 1 lemon, quartered
- 1 whole garlic head, cut in half
- 1 yellow onion, quartered
- 1 teaspoon salt
- ½ teaspoon black pepper
- 1 teaspoon rosemary
- 1 teaspoon thyme
- 1 tablespoon coconut oil

Directions

1. In a bowl mix the oil, herbs, salt and pepper. Rub this all over the chicken, on all sides, under wings and legs.

2. Put the garlic, onion and lemon inside of the chicken.

3. Put the chicken breast side down in cooker. (No liquid required)

4. Pull chicken out of cooker and put in oven safe ban under broiler to crisp skin if desired for 5-8 minutes.

5. Use the juices over potatoes or the chicken meat.

SLOW COOKER CHICKEN KORMA

Korma is a dish that originated in South Asia that has meat or veggies braised in a spicy sauce made with yogurt or cream. Here at GSDF we will use cashew cream instead of yogurt to keep it dairy free. The heat comes from the red pepper flakes. This dish is normally served over rice.

SERVES: 6 - 8; PREP TIME: 15 MINS; COOK TIME: 6 HRS LOW

Ingredients

- 2 pounds chicken, cut into cubes
- 1 yellow onion, diced
- 2 inches of ginger, peeled and diced
- 3 garlic cloves, minced
- 1 cinnamon stick
- 2 bay leaves
- 2 teaspoons curry powder
- 1 teaspoon coriander
- ½ teaspoon cumin
- ½ teaspoon crushed red pepper
- ½ cup cashew cream
- ⅓ cup water
- ½ bunch cilantro, chopped for garnish

Directions

1. In a blender put the onion, ginger, garlic and ⅓ cup of water. Puree until smooth.

2. Combine all the ingredients except the cashew cream and cilantro in a large bowl mixing well.

3. Pour into a slow cooker and cook on low 5 ½ hours.

4. Add the cashew cream and mix well, cook 30 minutes more.

5. Serve over rice and top with cilantro.

SLOW COOKER WHITE CHICKEN CHILI

A perfect healthy comfort dinner waiting for you when you get home when you use the slow cooker. This is a very easy dish to make but it has a wonderful layer of tasty flavors. I added a little of Southwestern flavor by using cumin, green chilies and cilantro. This is such an easy dish, all you have to do is add the ingredients and turn on your slow cooker. You will come home to a house full of delicious smells and warm bowls of mouth watering deliciousness!

SERVES: 6 - 8; PREP TIME: 15 MINS; COOK TIME: 4 - 6 HRS

Ingredients

- 4 boneless, skinless chicken breasts, cut into large chunks
- 1 yellow onion, diced
- 1 can diced fire roasted green chili peppers
- 4 cloves garlic, minced
- 2 teaspoons chili powder
- 1 teaspoons cumin
- 1 teaspoon salt
- ¼ teaspoon black pepper
- 1 teaspoon dried oregano
- 4 cups low-sodium chicken stock
- 1 can cannelloni , drained and rinsed
- ½ bunch cilantro, chopped

Directions

1. Combine the chicken, onions, green chili, garlic, cumin, chili powder, salt, oregano, black pepper, beans and stock in a 6-quart slow cooker.

2. Stir everything to mix well.

3. Place the lid on the slow cooker. Cook for 4 hours on high or 6 hours on low.

4. Serve in large bowls topped with the fresh cilantro.

Note: A squeeze of fresh lime is also delicious once cooked.

SOUTHWESTERN STUFFED BELL PEPPERS

I love stuffed bell peppers because it is a whole meal inside the edible pepper. Add a green side salad and dinner is done. I also like to take the left over stuffed bell peppers and slice them in half and put a fried egg over the half bell pepper, a great breakfast.

SERVES: 4; PREP TIME: 10 MINS; COOK TIME: 6 HRS LOW

Ingredients

- 4 bell peppers, tops removed, veins and seeds removed
- 1 pound ground beef
- 1 ½ cups wild rice, cooked
- 1 (15 oz) can fire roasted tomatoes
- 2 cups chicken stock
- 1 yellow onion, diced
- 4 cloves garlic, minced
- 1 (3 oz) can fire roasted green chilies
- 1 (5 oz) can corn kernels
- 1 (4 oz) can of tomato sauce
- 1 teaspoon cumin
- 1 teaspoon chili powder
- ½ teaspoon salt
- fresh black pepper

Directions

1. In a large bowl mix everything except ½ the fire roasted tomatoes, can of tomato sauce, the stock and bell peppers.

2. Stuff each bell pepper with ¼ of the mixture, stand them in the slow cooker, pour stock around the peppers, add the ½ can fire roasted tomatoes and tomato sauce, cover and cook for 6 hours on low.

SPICY GINGER LIME WINGS

SERVES: 4 - 6; PREP TIME: 10 MINS; COOK TIME: 3-4 HOURS

Ingredients

- 2 pounds chicken wings
- ¼ cup tamarri or coconut aminos
- ¼ cup balsamic vinegar
- 3 tablespoons honey (or stevia drops to taste)
- 4 cloves garlic, minced
- ½ teaspoon cayenne chili powder (more if you want super spicy)
- 2 teaspoons fresh grated ginger
- 3 tablespoons lime juice
- zest of one lime
- 2 teaspoons tapioca starch
- 2 teaspoons sesame seeds
- 2 tablespoons chopped chives

Directions

1. In a large bowl, whisk together coconut amino, balsamic vinegar, honey, garlic, cayenne chili powder, grated ginger, lime juice and lime zest.

2. Place wings into a slow cooker. Pour the sauce from the bowl over wings and mix well.

3. Cover and cook on low heat for 6 to 7 hours or high heat for 3 to 4 hours.

4. Near the end of cooking, in a small bowl, whisk together tapioca and one tablespoon water. Add mixture to slow cooker and stir.

5. Cover and cook on high heat for an additional 10 to 12 minutes, or until the sauce has thickened.

6. Serve immediately and garnish with sesame seeds and chives.

THAI CHICKEN AND VEGGIE RED CURRY

I love Thai red curry and doing it in the slow cooker makes it super simple to do! It comes out tasty. Add more red Thai curry paste for more spice. I actually use double than what the recipe calls for but I like mine on the spicy side.

PREP TIME: 15 MINS; COOK TIME: 4 HOURS LOW

Ingredients

- 2 boneless chicken breasts, cubed
- 2 zucchinis, cubed
- 1 bell pepper, diced
- 2 cups mushrooms, quartered
- 1 yellow onion, sliced
- 4 cloves garlic, minced
- 1 cup unsweetened coconut milk
- ½ cup chicken stock
- 1 tablespoon Thai red curry paste
- 1 tablespoon coconut oil

Directions

1. In a large skillet heat the coconut oil over medium high heat.

2. Sprinkle salt and pepper over the chicken and put into the skillet. Brown the chicken on all sides.

3. Add the chicken and the rest of the ingredients to the slow cooker. Stir to combine well, cover and cook on low for 4 hours.

WHITE CHICKEN CHILI

A perfect healthy comfort dinner waiting for you when you get home when you use the slow cooker. This is a very easy dish to make but it has a wonderful layer of tasty flavors. I added a little of Southwestern flavor by using cumin, green chilies and cilantro. This is such an easy dish, all you have to do is add the ingredients and turn on your slow cooker. You will come home to a house full of delicious smells and warm bowls of mouth watering deliciousness!

SERVES: 6 - 8; PREP TIME: 15 MINS; COOK TIME: 4-6 HOURS

Ingredients

- 4 boneless, skinless chicken breasts, cut into large chunks
- 1 yellow onion, diced
- 1 can diced fire roasted green chili peppers
- 4 cloves garlic, minced
- 2 teaspoons chili powder
- 1 teaspoons cumin
- 1 teaspoon salt
- ¼ teaspoon black pepper
- 1 teaspoon dried oregano
- 4 cups low-sodium chicken stock
- 1 can cannelloni , drained and rinsed
- ½ bunch cilantro, chopped

Directions

1. Combine the chicken, onions, green chili, garlic, cumin, chili powder, salt, oregano, black pepper, beans and stock in a 6-quart slow cooker.

2. Stir everything to mix well.

3. Place the lid on the slow cooker. Cook for 4 hours on high or 6 hours on low.

4. Serve in large bowls topped with the fresh cilantro.

Note: A squeeze of fresh lime is also delicious once cooked.

CHICKEN SOUPS

ASIAN CHICKEN SOUP

This soup is flavored with fresh ginger and garlic. Not only is it full of flavor but very good for you. I like to add a squeeze of lime or lemon when I serve it to bump up the flavor a bit. A perfect soup when you feel under the weather.

PREP TIME: 20 MINS; COOK TIME: 20 MINS

Ingredients

- 2 boneless skinless chicken breasts, sliced in thin strips
- 4 cups of stock
- ½ cup coconut amino, tamarai or gf soy
- 2 tablespoons fresh ginger, grated
- 4 cloves of garlic, grated
- 3 small bock choy, sliced
- 1 jalapeño, sliced in half
- 4 green onions, sliced thin
- 2 carrots, diced small
- ½ package thin rice sticks (6.75 ounce)
- 1 tablespoon coconut oil

Directions

1. In a large skillet over medium high heat, add the coconut oil and chicken. cook until cooked through, 5-8 minutes.

2. In a soup pot add the stock, chicken, tamari, ginger, garlic, jalapeño, carrots and cook for 10 minutes over medium low heat.

3. Add the noodles and and bock choy, simmer for 10 minutes.

4. Add the onions, remove the jalapeño and serve..

CHICKEN PHO

This chicken pho recipe is my version of a Vietnamese style soup that is full of flavor. The broth is infused with flavors of garlic, ginger and spices. Cooked rice noodles and tender strips of white chicken meat are added to the broth. Then you can choose to add fresh veggies and herbs. When you dine at a Vietnamese restaurant they will bring a platter piled high with cilantro, bean sprouts, basil, mint, green onions, watercress, thai red chilies and wedges of lime. The crunch of the bean sprouts and the fresh taste of the herbs compliments the broth, chicken and soft noodles. Traditionally the broth is a bone broth that takes a few days to make, my version is much easier and still has a lot of flavor.

SERVES: 4; PREP TIME: 15 MINS; COOK TIME: 25 MINS

Ingredients

- 4 cups chicken stock
- 2 cups water
- 3 inches fresh ginger, sliced
- 4 cloves garlic, sliced
- ½ yellow onion, sliced
- 4 teaspoons fish sauce
- 2 thai red chilies, sliced (jalapeño can substitute)
- 4 green onions, sliced
- ½ cup chopped cilantro
- ½ cup chopped mint

- 1 star anise
- ½ stick cinnamon
- ½ teaspoon turmeric
- 2 boneless skinless chicken breasts, sliced
- 2 tablespoons fresh lime juice
- ½ cup watercress
- 1 cup bean sprouts
- 2 limes, quartered
- 4 ounces rice noodles, cooked according to package instructions

Directions

1. In a sauce pan with a lid, add the stock, ginger, onion, garlic, fish sauce, star anise, cinnamon turmeric and 2 cups of water to a boil. Reduce heat to medium low, cover and simmer 15 minutes.

2. In another pot, bring 4 cups of water up to a boil, add the sliced chicken, lower the heat to medium low and poach for 10 minutes or until cooked. Drain and set aside.

3. Strain the broth mixture and return the liquid to the large pot. Add the chicken and lime juice and heat over medium low heat for 5 minutes.

4. Place the cooked noodles in the bottom of the bowls and ladle the broth mixture over them dividing it up evenly.

5. Put all the rest of the herbs and veggies on a large platter and serve with the soup.

6. Add your ingredients on top of the noodles and chicken, squeeze lime over the top and enjoy!.

CHICKEN STOCK

Ingredients

- Bones of a chicken
- Half a bunch of celery
- 4 carrots
- 1 onion quartered
- 6 cloves garlic
- 1 teaspoon black peppercorns
- 12 cups cold water
- ½ bunch parsley

Directions

1. Place all ingredients in a large stockpot and bring up to boil, simmer 2 hours, strain.

2. Put in big bowl in fridge with plastic wrap over night, skim fat off, put into storage containers.

3. Add salt and seasonings when ready to use Or

4. Take 2 pounds chicken wings, pound with a mallet toss with 3 tbl coconut oil, one onion quartered, 1/2 tea salt, and fresh black pepper. Toss, put on baking sheet 400 degree pre heated oven. Bake 150 minutes. Add to large stock pot as above and do the same as the recipe above.

CHICKEN TORTILLA SOUP

I love a good spicy chicken tortilla soup. This version is not spicy but has a lot of flavor so that the whole family can enjoy it. This is one of my go to soups when I have a cold or on a cold winters day.

The vibrant flavors and fresh veggies along with the avocado make this soup a one bowl meal.

It is easy to prepare and will cook on the stove with out a lot of work. Roasting bone in chicken breasts add a lot of flavor to both the chicken its self as well as the soup.

SERVES: 8; PREP TIME: 10 MINS; COOK TIME: 90 MINS

Ingredients

- 2 bone in chicken breasts, roasted
- 1 can fire roasted tomatoes
- 1 diced yellow onion
- 3 cloves garlic, minced
- ½ bell pepper, diced
- 1 can green chilies
- 3 tbl tomato paste
- 8 cups chicken stock
- 6 corn tortillas
- 1 tea chili powder
- 2 tea cumin
- ½ tea salt
- 1 tbl coconut oil
- 2 avocados
- ½ diced red onion
- 1 bunch cilantro, chopped
- 2 limes quartered

Directions

1. Preheat oven to 350 degrees.

2. Place chicken breast skin up on a baking sheet.

3. Season with a pinch of salt and cumin. Bake for 50 minutes. Set aside to cool.

4. Chop the onions, cilantro, garlic and bell pepper.

5. Heat the coconut oil in a large soup pot

6. Add the yellow onion, bell pepper and garlic.

7. Sauté until the onion is translucent about 5 minutes.

8. Add the cumin, chili powder and salt. Stir well

9. Then add the stock, green chilies and roasted tomatoes.

10. Using two forks shred the chicken meat and take off the bone.

11. Add to the soup.

12. Add the tomato paste and stir well.

13. Bring up to boil then lower to simmer and cook for 90 minutes uncovered.

14. While the soup is cooking, cut the corn tortillas into 2 inch strips.

15. Put on baking sheet and back into a 400 degree oven. Bake until crisp about 5- 7 minutes. (You

can also add the tortillas to the soup not toasted. Just add to the soup itself in the last 10 minutes of cooking so that they get super soft.)

16. Serve the soup in large bowls and top with the tortilla strips, avocado, red onion, cilantro and a squeeze of lime.

CHICKEN VEGGIE SOUP

This is a rustic soup with big chunks of vegetables, chicken and flavor. Don't let the list of ingredients spook you, it is a very easy soup to make and you can use what vegetables you have on hand.

SERVES: 6; PREP TIME: 15 MINS; COOK TIME: 30 MINS

Ingredients

- 1 tablespoon coconut oil
- 2 cloves garlic chopped
- ¼ cup good white wine
- 1-cup broccoli florets
- 2 small carrots peeled and diced
- ½ teaspoon dried oregano
- ½ can fire roasted tomatoes chopped
- ½ onion chopped
- 2 cups cooked chicken meat
- 6 baby bella mushrooms sliced
- 1 large handful baby spinach
- 1 cup green beans cut into one inch pieces
- 1 small zucchini diced
- 2 cups chicken or vegetable stock
- 3 small red potatoes diced
- fresh ground black pepper
- ½ to 1 teaspoon salt
- optional: ½ teaspoon herbs de provence

Directions

1. Sauté onions and garlic in olive oil, in a small pot, over medium heat, until translucent.
2. Add mushrooms and white wine.
3. Cook for 5 minutes over medium low heat so that the mushrooms can absorb most of the liquid and flavor.
4. Add rest of the ingredients including the liquid and seasonings all at once. Bring up to a bubble, lower the heat and partially cover for 20 minutes.

LEMON CHICKEN SOUP

This soup is one of my favorites, it has lots of lemon and roasted garlic in it. I love to make it if I feel a cold coming on! You can do it very quickly if you use a roast chicken you pick up at the market. I don't put noodles in this but if you wanted to use some rice noodles, add the cooked noodles the very end.

SERVES: 4; PREP TIME: 10 MINS; COOK TIME: 45 MINS

Ingredients

- 1 large head of garlic
- 6 cups chicken stock
- ½ cup fresh lemon juice (about 3 lemons)
- 1 lemon, sliced thinly
- 2 tablespoons fresh tarragon, chopped
- 2 boneless skinless chicken breasts
- 1 small yellow onion
- 1 carrot, peeled
- 1 bay leaf
- ½ teaspoon salt
- 2 teaspoons chili oil

Directions

1. Preheat the oven to 400 degrees F.

2. Cut the garlic head in half and rub olive oil over it with a pinch of salt.

3. Place cut side down on a piece of foil and wrap up tight. Bake for 30 minutes. Then set aside to cool.

4. Add the stock to a pot and bring up to a boil and then simmer.

5. Add the onion, peeled and cut in half, the carrot, bay leaf and salt.

6. Cut the chicken into thin strips and add to the stock. Simmer on low heat for 30 minutes.

7. Strain the soup separating the chicken from the veggies.

8. Squeeze the soft garlic coves from the roasted half heads with your fingers into a new sauce pan.

9. Whist 1 cup of the stock into the pan to loosen the garlic paste and get it incorporated.

10. Add the rest of the stock, lemon juice and chopped tarragon. Bring to a boil and lower to a simmer.

11. Add the chicken to the pot. Cover and cook 15 minutes.

12. Garnish the soup with the thin slices of the lemons and ½ teaspoon chili oil.

THAI CHICKEN COCONUT SOUP (TOM KHA GAI)

I love Thai food so much that I decided years ago to learn how to make it. I got to study with well known Chef Chat Mingkwan in Sonoma California. I learned so much from him about Thai cooking. The hardest part about preparing the meal is all of the prep work. So many steps go into creating the curry pastes, the broths, the dressings, the marinades and more.

My goal is to take those traditional Thai flavor profiles and make it easy for the home cook to recreate the dish. Tom Kha Gai, Thai chicken coconut soup is one of my go to soups when I want to make something quick, spicy and delicious.

The soup traditionally calls for kaffir lime leaves which add the unique lime flavor but in this version we will use lime. I also use ginger instead of galangal. Yet if you can find these items locally, use the traditional ones!

This recipe calls for lemongrass but if you can not find it, substitute zest of a lemon and ½ teaspoon grated ginger.

SERVES: 4 - 6; PREP TIME: 15 MINS; COOK TIME: 20 MINS

Ingredients

- 2 inch piece of ginger, sliced into thin rings
- 4 cups good chicken stock
- 1 can unsweetened coconut milk
- 1 lime, zested
- ¼ cup fresh lime juice
- 2 tablespoons fish sauce (3 crabs brand)
- 1 tablespoon coconut sugar
- 2 thai red chilis or jalapeño chiles, cut length wise
- 1 ½ cups thinly sliced cooked chicken
- 8 ounces shiitake, oyster, baby bella mushrooms, thinly sliced
- 2 lemongrass stalks, smashed with knife and then cut into 2" pieces
- ¼ cup fresh cilantro chopped for garnish
- chili oil optional

Directions

1. In a large soup pan, put the broth, lemongrass, chilies and ginger into the pan. Bring up to boil, reduce heat and simmer for 10 minutes. Then strain the soup taking out the solids.

2. Add the cooked chicken and mushrooms to the stock and cook over medium heat for 10 minutes.

3. Add the coconut milk, fish sauce and sugar. cook for 10 more minutes. Serve and garnish with cilantro.

4. Sprinkle some chili oil over the top of the soup if you want more spice.

CHICKEN ON THE STOVETOP

CHICKEN FAJITAS

Chicken fajitas is a quick dish that is very easy to make and has tons of flavor. I love eating mine in butter lettuce leaves but corn tortillas work great also. I also like to use red, yellow and orange bell peppers since they add a lot of color, nutrients and are much sweeter than green bell peppers. Add some fresh salsa or some guacamole and you have a feast on your hands!

SERVES: 4 - 6; PREP TIME: 20 MINS; COOK TIME: 15 MINS

Ingredients

- 2 pounds of chicken breasts, cut into strips
- 3 bell peppers
- 2 onions
- 2 teaspoons oregano
- 2 teaspoons chili powder
- 2 teaspoons cumin
- 3 cloves of garlic, minced
- 2 lemons, juiced
- 1 lime, juiced
- 1 jalapeño, seeded and minced
- 1 tablespoon coconut oil
- 1 bunch of cilantro

Directions

1. Take ¼ of the bunch of cilantro and chop the leaves, removing the stems and set aside.

2. In a blender add the rest of the cilantro (stems included), oregano, chili powder, cumin, garlic, lemon juice, lime juice and the jalapeño. Blend until smooth.

3. Cut the chicken into strips.

4. Seed and cut the bell peppers into strips.

5. Slice the onions into strips.

6. In a large bowl, combine the chicken, peppers, onions and the mixture from the blender and mix well. Cover and put in fridge for 2-4 hours.

7. In a large frying pan, heat the coconut oil.

8. Add the chicken mixture to the pan. Cook making sure to stir and turn the ingredients over in the pan. Cook for 6-9 minutes or until done.

9. Sprinkle the chopped, reserved cilantro over the chicken.

10. Serve with butter lettuce leaves or corn tortillas.

CHICKEN KORMA

Korma is a dish that originated in South Asia that has meat or veggies braised in a spicy sauce made with yogurt or cream. Here at GSDF we will use cashew cream instead of yogurt to keep it dairy free. The heat comes from the red pepper flakes. This dish is normally served over rice.

SERVES: 6 - 8; PREP TIME: 15 MINS; COOK TIME: 40 MINS

Ingredients

- 2 pounds chicken, cut into cubes
- 1 yellow onion, diced
- 2 inches of ginger, peeled and diced
- 3 garlic cloves, minced
- 1 cinnamon stick
- 2 bay leaves
- 2 teaspoons curry powder
- 1 teaspoon coriander
- ½ teaspoon cumin
- ½ teaspoon crushed red pepper
- ½ cup cashew cream
- ⅓ cup water
- ½ bunch cilantro, chopped for garnish

Directions

1. In a blender put the onion, ginger, garlic and ⅓ cup of water. Puree until smooth.

2. Combine all the ingredients except the cilantro in a large dutch oven. Bring up to heat and then simmer, uncovered 35 minutes stirring occasionally. Add more water if it gets too thick.

3. Serve over rice and top with cilantro.

CHICKEN PICCATA

Chicken Piccata is traditionally a lemon butter sauce with capers. In this GSDF version you never miss the butter, the sauce is still tangy and delicious. I love to make extra sauce to pour over the steamed broccoli I usually serve with this dish.

SERVES: 4; PREP TIME: 15 MINS; COOK TIME: 20 MINS

Ingredients

- 4 boneless skinless chicken breasts
- 1 lemon
- 2 tablespoons coconut oil
- 1-cup coconut flour or gluten free flour mix
- ⅓ cup lemon juice (1-2 lemons)
- ½ cup chicken stock
- 3 Tbsp. capers
- 2 Tbsp. chopped parsley
- pinch of Salt
- pinch of Pepper

Directions

1. Butterfly the chicken breasts or purchase the thin cut chicken breasts and sprinkle with salt and pepper.

2. Dredge the chicken in the coconut flour and shaking off the excess.

3. Juice the lemons.

4. Heat coconut oil in large frying pan over medium heat Add the chicken to the skillet not crowding it and doing it in two batches. When the side is brown flip and cook other side about 5 minutes total. Remove from the pan and put on plate covered with foil to keep warm.

5. Do the second batch of chicken breasts and set aside.

6. In the pan put the lemon juice, stock and capers. Stir and scrape up any brown bits. Cook over low heat at a simmer for 5 min.

7. Add the chicken back to the pan to warm through. 2-3 minutes.

8. Serve the chicken pouring the sauce over the chicken and topping with chopped parsley.

CHICKEN TENDERS

This Caribbean black bean soup is a tasty, spicy bowl of flavor. I added thyme, cumin, ginger, allspice and chili to the base. At the end coconut milk and lime juice is added to marry all the flavors together. Bell peppers, black beans and chunks of fire roasted tomatoes soak up all the flavors that will have your taste buds dancing.

SERVES: 4 - 6; PREP TIME: 15 MINS; COOK TIME: 20 MINS

Ingredients

- 2 lb chicken tenderloins
- 1 cup coconut flour
- 1 tsp paprika
- ½ tsp garlic powder
- ½ tsp salt
- ¼ tsp poultry seasoning
- 2 eggs
- 1-2 tablespoons coconut oil

Directions

1. Preheat oven to 425.

2. Use a shallow dish to combine coconut flour with the poultry seasoning.

3. In another shallow dish crack the two eggs beat until combined.

4. Lay one piece of chicken in egg and flip to thoroughly cover. Remove from eggs and dip chicken in dry ingredients, flipping to cover entire piece. Shake off excess.

5. Place in baking dish that has been rubbed with coconut oil. Repeat with remaining chicken pieces.

6. Bake for 8 minutes.

7. Turn chicken pieces over and bake for another 8 minutes or until browned.

CHICKEN WITH ZUCCHINI NOODLES

This zucchini noodle and chicken dish has bright flavors from garlic, cumin, chili powder and fresh lime juice. It is a fresh take on a healthy dish. I have become a huge fan of zucchini noodles. They are so much fun to make, quick to cook and tasty to eat. I love to let my garlic simmer in the coconut oil before quickly tossing the noodles in so that the noodles soak up the garlic flavor.

SERVES: 4; PREP TIME: 15 MINS; COOK TIME: 20 MINS

Ingredients

- 2 boneless, skinless chicken breasts, cut into 1" pieces
- 3 large zucchini, made into noodles
- 1 red bell pepper, seeded and cut into thin strips
- 1 clove garlic, minced
- ½ teaspoon ground cumin
- ½ teaspoon chili powder
- 1 teaspoon salt, divided
- ¼ teaspoon fresh ground black pepper
- 1 large lime
- 2 tablespoons coconut oil, divided

Directions

1. Sprinkle the chicken pieces with ½ teaspoon salt, pepper, chili powder and the cumin, toss to coat well.

2. Either use a spiralizer or mandolin to make zucchini noodles or cut into very thin strips with a sharp knife.

3. In a large skillet over medium high heat, melt the coconut milk. Add the chicken and cook until done, about 7-10 minutes making sure that it is cooked through and on all sides. Put on a plate and set aside.

4. Wipe out the pan and put over medium high heat. Add the coconut oil and once it melts, add the garlic, turn heat down very low and simmer for 5 minutes to infuse the oil with the garlic flavor, making sure not to burn.

5. Add the zucchini noodles and bell peppers and toss in oil, coating evenly. Sauté for 2 minutes while stirring gently. Add the chicken, salt and juice of the lime, stir well and serve warm.

CHIPOTLE CHICKEN

A chipotle is a smoked jalapeño that comes in a small can in adobo sauce. This simple ingredient can transform a dish with its smokey spicy notes. This dish calls for a sauce made with the chipotle in adobo sauce, tomato sauce, onions, cumin, garlic and chili powder.It is an easy one dish meal that has a lot of flavor..

SERVES: 4; PREP TIME: 5 MINS; COOK TIME: 25 MINS

Ingredients

- 4 boneless skinless chicken breast halves
- 2 teaspoons cumin, divided
- ½ teaspoon chili powder
- 1 teaspoon salt. Divided
- ¼ teaspoon pepper
- ½ to 1 medium chipotle chile in adobo sauce, minced
- 2 teaspoons adobo sauce
- 2 garlic cloves, minced
- ½ onion thinly sliced
- ½ cup tomato sauce
- 4 tablespoons chopped fresh cilantro, divided
- 2 teaspoons coconut oil
- 2 roma tomatoes

Directions

1. Combine 1 teaspoon cumin, chili powder and salt in small bowl and then sprinkle over chicken on both sides.

2. Combine chipotle chile, adobo sauce, minced garlic, sliced onion, tomato sauce, roma tomatoes, 1 teaspoon cumin and ½ teaspoon salt into a small pan and let simmer over medium heat for 10 minutes. Tasting sauce for salt and pepper.

3. Heat coconut oil in large nonstick skillet over medium-high heat until it melts, coating the bottom of the skillet. Add seasoned chicken breasts to pan making sure not to over lap.

4. Cook chicken 4 minutes or until browned on one side. Turn chicken breasts over and top with the tomato sauce mixture.

5. Reduce heat to medium-low; simmer, covered, 10-15 minutes or until chicken is no longer pink in center. Remove from heat. Stir 3 tablespoons of the cilantro into sauce.

6. Serve chicken with sauce over it and top with remaining cilantro.

GINGER CHICKEN AND NOODLE BOWL

I found that I could get gluten free ramen noodles and this dish came together quickly with ingredients I had on hand. I have also made this dish using miracle noodles, zucchini noodles and even served it over rice. it is your choice but you want to have something to soak up the ginger sesame sauce!

SERVES: 4; PREP TIME: 15 MINS; COOK TIME: 15 MINS

Ingredients

- 1 pound chicken breasts, cut into 1-inch pieces
- 1 red bell pepper, cut into pieces
- 5-6 small bok toy cut into pieces
- 2 tablespoons fresh chopped ginger
- 2 cloves garlic, minced
- ½ cup chicken stock
- 3 tablespoons tamari or gluten free soy sauce
- ½ teaspoon sesame oil
- ½ teaspoon crushed red pepper flakes
- ½ teaspoon rice vinegar
- 2 tablespoons coconut oil
- 1 box ramen noodles

Directions

1. Cook the ramen noodles according to the package, rinse and set aside.

2. In a large frying pan heat the coconut oil.

3. Add the bok choy and the bell pepper. Sauté for 4 minutes and remove to a plate.

4. Add the chicken, garlic and ginger to the pan and cook until the chicken is cooked through about 4 minutes.

5. Then add the bok choy, bell pepper and all the rest of the ingredients. Stirling to mix well. Let it cook down a little about 4 minutes.

6. If you desire the sauce a little thicker add ½ teaspoon corn starch to 2 table spoons of stock, mix well and then add to the pan. Cook for a few minutes as it thickens.

GINGER MUSHROOM CHICKEN

The sauce is made of tamarin, stock, vinegar, ginger and green onions. It cooks super fast and is full of flavor. A perfect meal when you are in a rush!

SERVES: 4; PREP TIME: 10 MINS; COOK TIME: 15 MINS

MARINADE

Ingredients

- ⅓ cup tamari or coconut aminos
- ¾ cup chicken stock
- 3 tbs rice vinegar
- 3 tbs corn starch
- ⅓ tea black pepper
- 2 green onions cut into one inch pieces
- 2 tsp ground ginger

MAIN DISH

Ingredients

- 1 pound of boneless skinless chicken breasts
- 2 garlic cloves, minced
- 1 tablespoon coconut oil
- 1 cup baby bella mushrooms, halved
- 1 cup shiitake mushrooms, stems removed and halved
- 3 cups baby kale or chopped kale

Directions

1. In a zip bag add all the ingredients for the marinade, seal and shake to mix. Reserve ¼ cup in a separate container.

2. Thinly slice the chicken and add it to the marinade. Let it marinade for 2 hours.

3. In a large skillet or wok, add the coconut oil and let it melt. Add the chicken and cook it though 4-5 minutes, put on a plate to rest.

4. Add the mushrooms and garlic to the skillet, cook 3 minutes.

5. Add reserved marinade and cook 3-4 more minutes.

6. Then add the kale until it wilts about 3 minutes.

7. Add the chicken to the skillet and warm through, about 2-3 minutes.

8. Serve over rice or quinoa.

GOURMET CHICKEN STROGANOFF

My happy place is in recipe creation, food flavor profiles and in the kitchen. So after a stressful day, I had a craving for a big bowl of beef stroganoff. I decided to indulge my desire and create a gluten dairy free version that would still taste delicious, be comforting and enjoyable. When I went to the kitchen to crate my new dish, I only had chicken on hand. So my gourmet chicken stroganoff was created.

SERVES: 4; PREP TIME: 10 MINS; COOK TIME: 35 MINS

Ingredients

- 3 tablespoons coconut oil divided
- 1 small yellow onion or half of a normal one diced
- 1-2 diced cloves of garlic
- 4-5 fresh shiitake mushrooms sliced
- 1/3 cup of diced chanterelle mushrooms
- 1/2 cup good white wine
- 1/2 cup good chicken stock
- 1/4 cup coconut milk
- 1/2 teaspoon thyme
- 1/2 teaspoon salt
- 1/4 teaspoon fresh ground black pepper
- 1 large boneless skinless chicken breast or 2 normal size ones sliced
- 1 package gluten free pasta cooked

Directions

1. Heat 2 tablespoons of coconut oil in a large skillet on medium heat. Add the diced onions and garlic and sauce until translucent.

2. Add the sliced and diced mushrooms and cook until mushrooms are tender. Cook for about 3 minutes.

3. Add the white wine and cook 2-3 minutes until the wine is almost completely evaporated.

4. Add the stock, coconut milk, thyme, salt and pepper.

5. In another small frying pan, add the coconut oil and cook over medium heat the strips of chicken breast until done. This takes about 2 minutes a side.

6. Add the cooked chicken to the sauce. Bring up to a boil and then lower to simmer for 10 minutes stirring occasionally. The sauce will thicken naturally

7. Add the cooked pasta to the sauce and mix well.

8. Let cook together for 2 minutes so that the noodles soak up the flavorful sauce.

HERB CHICKEN MEATBALLS

These chicken meatballs are packed full of fresh herbs and flavors. Good as is but fantastic in the Vegan Basil Cream Sauce.

Ingredients

- 2 pounds ground chicken
- 3 ounces finely chopped pancetta
- ½ cup gf breadcrumbs
- 1 teaspoon chopped rosemary
- 2 teaspoons chopped thyme
- 2 tablespoons chopped parsley
- 3 tablespoons minced shallot
- 4 garlic cloves, minced
- 3 tablespoons grated carrot
- 1 large egg, lightly beaten
- 1 ½ teaspoons salt Freshly ground black pepper
- 2-4 tablespoons coconut oil

Directions

1. Place the ground chicken and pancetta in a large glass or stainless steel bowl.

2. Add breadcrumbs, rosemary, thyme, 2 tablespoons parsley, shallot and garlic. Mix well.

3. With your fingers gently, do not over mix.

4. Season with salt and a few grinds of pepper then add the egg and mix well.

5. Let the mixture sit for 10 minutes.

6. Heat a large sauté pan over medium high heat. When the pan is hot, add enough coconut oil to lightly coat the bottom.

7. Immediately add 10 to 12 meatballs to the pan. Allow room between the meatballs so that you can move them around easily to brown on all sides.

8. Let the meatballs sear for a couple of minutes before turning.

9. Then the meatballs are golden on all sides remove them to a sheet pan.

10. Repeat until all the meatballs are browned.

11. Place the pan in the oven and roast for 15 to 20 minutes until cooked through.

LEMON CHICKEN ZOODLES

I love the flavor of lemon and chicken together. This zoodle dish is extra tasty since the coconut oil gets infused with garlic and then the noodles are cooked in the garlic oil. A delicious quick easy meal.

SERVES: 4; PREP TIME: 15 MINS; COOK TIME: 15 MINS

Ingredients

- 2 boneless skinless chicken breasts, cut into strips
- 4 medium zucchini
- 2 cloves garlic, minced
- 3 Roma tomatoes, diced
- 1 lemon, juiced and zested
- ½ teaspoon oregano
- ¼ teaspoon salt
- a few grinds fresh black pepper
- pinch of red pepper flakes
- 3 tablespoons coconut oil, divided

Directions

1. In a large skillet add 2 tablespoons coconut oil and minced garlic, lower the flame to low and let it simmer for 5 minutes.

2. Use a spiralizer to make the zoodles or a sharp knife.

3. Sprinkle salt and pepper over the chicken pieces. In another skillet add the coconut oil over medium high heat. Once the oil has melted, add the chicken and cook util it is fully cooked, 6-8 minutes. Set aside.

4. In the skillet with the garlic oil add the tomatoes and cook for 1 minute. Add the zoodles tossing them gently in the garlic oil. Cook 2-3 minutes.

5. Add the chicken, lemon zest, lemon juice, oregano, salt, pepper and red pepper flakes and mix well.

6. Serve right away.

PAPRIKA CHICKEN

Paprika Chicken is also known as Hungarian Paprika Chicken. This dish has tomato paste, cashew cream, tender pieces of chicken, red bell pepper and onions. It is wonderful served over gf noodles or rice. Now you can enjoy the creamy goodness of the dish without dairy. This is a super easy dish to make but your dinner guests will think it came from a 5 star restaurant! Try something new tonight, it might become your new family favorite!.

SERVES: 4 - 6; PREP TIME: 15 MINS; COOK TIME: 80 MINS

Ingredients

- 3 pounds boneless skinless chicken breasts, cubed
- ½ teaspoon salt
- ½ teaspoon freshly ground pepper
- 2 tablespoons coconut oil
- 1 yellow onion, diced
- 1 red bell pepper, diced
- 2 tablespoons tomato paste
- 2 tablespoons sweet paprika
- 1 teaspoon crushed red pepper
- 1 teaspoon dried marjoram
- 1 ½ cups chicken stock
- ⅓ cup cashew cream
- 2 tablespoons fresh parsley, finely minced

Directions

7. Put all the ingredients except the quinoa and fresh basil into the slow cooker, mix well, cover and cook for 6 ½ hours.

8. Stir in the cooked quinoa, cover, cook 30 minutes.

9. Serve with strips of fresh basil leaves on top.

POACHED GINGER CHICKEN

This poached ginger chicken is perfect to toss in with zucchini sesame noodles for a quick dinner or chop the chicken into pieces and make a chicken salad. When you poach a chicken whole this way the meat is tender, moist and flavorful.

Ingredients

- One whole chicken
- 3 inch long piece of fresh ginger
- 1 bunch of green onion
- 4 carrots
- 3 stalks fresh basil
- 4 quarts organic chicken stock
- 1 tablespoon fresh black peppercorns
- Salt
- Pepper

Directions

1. Peel the ginger using the front part of a spoon, it comes off easily this way. Slice the ginger into $\frac{1}{4}$ inch size rings.

2. Cut the green onions into 1 inch pieces

3. Cut the carrots leaving the skin on into one inch pieces.

4. Rinse and pat dry the chicken. Season the chicken inside and out with salt and pepper.

5. Place the chicken, carrots, onion, ginger, basil, peppercorns and stock in a large stock pot making sure that the chicken is submerged in the liquid. Add water if needed to cover the chicken.

6. Cover and bring to a low simmer over medium heat. Reduce the heat to low and simmer for 30 minutes.

7. Turn the heat off, not disturbing the lid so that it can stay warm and let it stand for 30 minutes or up to 1 hour for the chicken to finish cooking.

8. Remove the chicken, carve, and serve.

9. Strain the broth and remove the fat. The chicken can be eaten warm or sliced up for other uses. The broth is perfect for soups.

SPINACH AND MUSHROOM STUFFED CHICKEN BREASTS

When I first wrote my recipe for stuffed chicken breasts it was for my cookbook: Family Favorites for One. I had used spinach, mushrooms, provolone cheese and a ton of wine. This is my easier version that still has the same flavor profile and is easy to make.

SERVES: 4; PREP TIME: 15 MINS; COOK TIME: 20 MINS

Ingredients

- 4 boneless skinless chicken breasts
- 2 cups fresh spinach
- 2 garlic cloves, minced
- 1 cup crimini mushrooms, finely chopped
- 3 tablespoons coconut oil
- ¼ yellow onion, diced
- ½ teaspoon red pepper flakes
- ½ teaspoon salt
- fresh ground pepper
- ¼ cup white wine
- ½ cup chicken stock

Directions

1. In a large dry skillet, cook the spinach until wilted and sprinkle with a pinch of salt. Squeeze out the water and add to a bowl.

2. In a large skillet melt 1 tablespoon of the coconut oil.

3. Add to the skillet the onion, garlic and mushrooms. Cook for about 3-5 minutes over medium heat until done. Add to the spinach.

4. Once the spinach mixture has cooled mix ingredients well.

5. Cut a horizontal slit through the chicken to create a pocket

6. Divide the spinach mix in half and stuff each breast and close the pockets with toothpicks.

7. Sprinkle the breasts with the salt, red pepper flakes and pepper evenly on both sides.

8. Add the 2 tablespoons of coconut oil to the skillet over medium heat.

9. Add the chicken breasts. Cook 4 minutes and then turn over. Add the wine and stock mix to the pan. Cover and cook 5 minutes.

10. Remove the lid and cook another 2-4 minutes until chicken is done and sauce is reduced.

11. Serve chicken with sauce poured over.

THAI CHICKEN AND ZOODLE BOWL

This Thai chicken and zoodle bowl is packed full of flavor. The noodles are made with carrots and zucchini and tossed with shredded chicken, red bell pepper, bean sprouts, cilantro and nuts all tossed in a lovely creamy nut sauce.

SERVES: 4; PREP TIME: 20 MINS; COOK TIME: 3 MINS

Ingredients

FOR THE DRESSING:

- 4 tablespoons nut butter
- ¼ cup coconut milk
- ¼ teaspoon cayenne chile
- 1 lime, juiced
- 1 tablespoon coconut aminos or tamari

- 4 medium zucchinis
- 4 carrots, peeled
- 3 cups cooked chicken, shredded
- 4 green onions, sliced thin
- 1 cup bean sprouts
- ½ bunch cilantro, chopped
- 1 red bell pepper, thinly sliced
- ¼ cup nuts (almond slivers or chopped peanuts)

Directions

1. In a small bowl mix the nut butter, coconut milk, chili, lime and coconut aminos and set aside.

2. Using a spiralizer (or a very sharp knife) made noodles out of the zucchini and carrots.

3. In a large skillet add the dressing, noodles and chicken. Toss to mix and keep tossing as it heats up and starts to cook, 2-3 minutes. Add the onions, bean sprouts, cilantro and nuts, toss and serve right away.

THAI CHICKEN STIR-FRY

I love the flavors of Thai food and I also love making quick dinners when I am tired! This recipe is an easy but tasty way to incorporate the bold and fresh tastes of Thai food. I love the texture and flavor of it in this dish.

SERVES: 4; PREP TIME: 15 MINS; COOK TIME: 15 MINS

Ingredients

- 4 tablespoons coconut oil, divided
- 1 pound chicken tenders cut into 2 inch sized pieces
- 1 jalapeño finely minced
- 1 bunch green onions thinly sliced
- 2 cups sliced shitake mushrooms
- 1 cup coconut milk
- 1 tablespoons minced ginger or ½ teaspoon ginger powder
- 2 tablespoons fish sauce
- juice of 1 lime
- 2 tablespoons coconut sugar
- 5 cups thinly sliced Napa cabbage
- 1 cup fresh basil, cut into ribbons

Directions

1. Mince the jalapeño. For less spice remove the ribs and seeds.

2. Peel and mince ginger. Using a spoon to peel fresh ginger is the easiest way.

3. Slice the Napa cabbage into thin strips and the same with the fresh basil, set aside.

4. Thinly slice the green onions separating the green and white parts. Slice the shiitake mushrooms and set aside.

5. Preheat a medium sauté pan on the stove and then add 2 teaspoons of the coconut oil.

6. Once the oil is hot, add the chicken pieces to the pan and sauté for 3-4 minutes or until golden brown on all sides.

7. Remove from pan keep warm on a covered plate.

8. Add remaining coconut oil to the pan and heat.

9. Add jalapeño, the white part of onion, the mushrooms and ginger, sauté for 2 minutes.

10. Add the coconut milk, fish sauce, lime juice and coconut sugar, bring up to heat and then simmer for 5-8 minutes or until the mushrooms are cooked.

11. Stir in the cabbage, chicken and green part of onions. Cook until cabbage is wilted, about 2-3 minutes.

12. Remove from heat , stir in the fresh basil and serve.

THAI MANGO CHICKEN CURRY

This is one of my favorite dishes to make when I find nice ripe mango at the market. I wrote it for 2 servings but it doubles and triples very well.

This dish has a little bit of heat and a touch of sweet. I usually serve this over brown rice or quinoa. I like to use chicken stock instead of water when making rice or quinoa so it has a lot more flavor.

SERVES: 2; PREP TIME: 15 MINS; COOK TIME: 30 MINS

Ingredients

- 1 large or 2 small chicken breasts
- 1 large ripe mango
- 1 tablespoon fish sauce
- 1-2 teaspoons red curry paste (the more, the spicier)
- ½ red bell pepper diced
- ¾ cup coconut milk
- ¾ cup chicken stock
- 1 tablespoon chopped cilantro

Directions

1. Stir together the chicken stock, coconut milk, fish sauce and red curry paste over medium heat in a sauce pan and bring up to heat. Then let it

simmer as the curry paste incorporates into the liquid, stirring occasionally.

2. Cut the chicken into 2-inch pieces.

3. Dice the bell pepper.

4. When chopping a mango there is an easier way! Cut the large sides off using your knife following along the smooth side of the large flat pit. Once the mango is cut off the seed, use a large spoon to scoop the meat out from the thick peel in one piece. Now you can chop the mango into similar pieces. Do this for each side and then dice the mango.

5. Once the red curry paste has integrated into the stock, add the mango, chicken and bell pepper.

6. Bring it up to a boil and immediately lower the heat to simmer for 20 minutes.

7. Once the curry is done, serve over your favorite brown rice or quinoa and sprinkle the chopped cilantro over the top of the dish.

ALL TURKEY

ASIAN TURKEY MEATBALLS

These meatballs pack a bunch of great Asian inspired flavor and are a great meal wrapped in a nice lettuce leaf with some of the dressing drizzled over them. I like to make them mini sized so they fit nicely in the lettuce wraps and they don't dry out during cooking. The trick with ground turkey or ground chicken is to keep the meat moist and add tons of flavor. This recipe does exactly that.

SERVES: 4; PREP TIME: 15 MINS; COOK TIME: 8 MINS

Ingredients

FOR THE DRESSING:

- 2 tablespoon fish sauce
- 2 tablespoon rice vinegar
- 2 teaspoons sesame oil
- ½ teaspoon red pepper flakes
- ½ teaspoon coconut sugar
- juice of 1 lime

FOR THE MEATBALLS:

- 1 pound ground turkey
- 1 teaspoon garlic
- 1 tablespoon fresh grated ginger
- 1 teaspoon sesame oil
- 2 teaspoon rice vinegar
- 1 teaspoon tamari or coconut aminos sauce
- 2 teaspoon coconut oil for cooking
- 2 tbspn shredded carrots

FOR THE GARNISH:

- Cucumber
- red bell pepper strips
- shredded carrots
- mint or cilantro
- lettuce leaves
- Instructions

Directions

1. To make the dressing combine fish sauce, rice vinegar, sesame oil, red pepper flakes, coconut sugar and lime juice in small mixing bowl.

2. Whisk until incorporated. Set aside.

3. Prep your garnish by separating the lettuce leaves, rinse and pat dry. Set aside

4. Dice the cucumber. Set aside

5. Mince herbs. Set aside

6. For your meatballs; mince the garlic. Set aside

7. Grate the ginger. Set aside

8. In large mixing bowl combine ground turkey, garlic, ginger, sesame oil, rice vinegar and soy sauce.

9. Stir until just combined, being careful not to over stir and create tough meatballs

10. Use tablespoon to measure mix and form into balls using your hands.

11. Heat oil in large skillet on medium heat.

12. Once the oil is hot, add meatballs.

13. Brown on all sides, cooking for a total of 5-7mins.

14. Garnish and serve.

HERB ROASTED TURKEY

The wow factor and flavor factor of stuffing the herbs under the skin in coconut milk is fantastic, and it makes for a tasty moist turkey.

PREP TIME: 20 MINS; COOK TIME: 20 MINS A POUND UNTIL IT REACHES 165 DEGREES

Ingredients

- 1 large turkey
- 1 lemon
- 1 head garlic
- 2 sprigs rosemary
- ½ bunch of thyme
- ½ yellow onion
- 1 box of organic chicken stock
- 2 cups good white wine or water
- salt and pepper
- Coconut Herb Mix

Directions

1. Pre heat oven to 350 degrees

2. Put frozen turkey in fridge for 4-5 days to defrost.

3. Rinse the turkey under cold water removing the neck, heart and giblets. Pat dry with paper towels.

4. Cut the onion into slivers, cut the garlic head in half, slice the lemon into slices and set aside.

5. Sprinkle salt and pepper inside and all over the outside of the turkey.

6. In a large bowl put the lemon slices, garlic halves, onion slices, thyme stalks and sprigs of rosemary and toss well.

7. Stuff the inside of the turkey with the lemon mixture. (This adds tons of flavor to the meat and helps to keep it moist)

8. Take the disks of the coconut herb mix and put under the skin of the breast and legs of the turkey making sure to get it all the way under and cover all the breast meat. This will melt, keep the breast moist and the herbs will infuse the meat with great flavor.

9. Saving two of the disks and rub the outside of the turkey with the herb coconut oil mix.

10. Place turkey on roasting rack in a large roasting pan. Pour the stock and wine under the bird. Put into oven.

11. After an hour make sure to baste the bird every 20 minutes using the liquid below the turkey. If it gets low, add more stock and wine.

12. When the legs and top get brown, make a tent out of foil and lightly cover the top to protect it.

13. Removing the tent to baste and putting it back after.

14. Once the turkey reaches 165 degrees remove from the oven, put the turkey in its roasting rack on a cutting board, cover all over with foil and then with two bath towels. Let stand 45 minutes. Uncover, and let stand 15 minutes. Then it is ready to carve. This will ensure a moist turkey.

15. Keep the drippings in the roasting pan and add the make ahead gravy to it stirring and tasting for salt and pepper.

HERB COCONUT OIL MIX

PREP TIME: 15 MINS; FREEZE TIME: OVERNIGHT

Ingredients

- 1 cup coconut oil, soft not melted
- 2 tablespoons chopped basil leaves
- 2 tablespoons chopped parsley leaves
- 2 tablespoons chopped sage leaves
- 1 tablespoon chopped thyme leaves
- 1 teaspoon chopped rosemary leaves
- 4 cloves garlic, minced
- 1 teaspoon salt

Directions

1. Chop all of the herbs very fine. Put into bowl and toss together.

2. Mince the garlic and add to herb mix and toss.

3. Add the soft coconut oil and salt, mix well

4. Put mix onto a piece of parchment paper and shape into a round log. Twist the ends and freeze over night.

5. When ready to use, slice the log into ¼ inch thick discs and place under the skin of the turkey.

NOTE: This is my version of compound butter. I use coconut oil instead. As the mixture melts under the skin of the bird, the flavor infuses into the meat.

6. When you slice the meat, you will have a crispy skin, layer of herbs and then the juice meat for a great wow factor and fantastic taste.

7. Make sure to put this mix under the skin of the breasts and both of the legs

THAI TURKEY SALAD

This Thai inspired Turkey Salad has fresh lime and mint leaves for extra flavor. The crunch of the Napa cabbage, carrots, green onions, bell pepper and cucumber make this a delicious refreshing salad base. The ground turkey is flavored with a little coconut sugar, lime, fish sauce and chili flakes.

SERVES: 4; PREP TIME: 15 MINS; COOK TIME: 10 MINS

Ingredients

- 1 pound ground turkey
- 4 cups shredded Napa cabbage
- 2 carrots grated or spiralized
- 4 cups green onions, sliced thin green and white part
- 1 red bell pepper, cut into thin strips
- ½ English cucumber, diced
- 1 tablespoons coconut sugar
- 2 tablespoons fish sauce
- ½ teaspoon red chili flakes
- ½ cup fresh mint leaves, torn
- ½ cup chopped peanuts or almond slices
- 2 tablespoons fresh lime juice
- 1 tablespoon coconut oil
- lime wedges, for serving

Directions

1. In a large skillet over medium high heat, melt the coconut oil. Add the turkey and cook it while breaking it up with a spatula. Cook all the way though 4-5 minutes.

2. Add the fish sauce, coconut sugar, chili flakes and ¼ cup water to the skillet. Cook 3-4 minutes until the liquid is absorbed.

3. In a large bowl, toss the cabbage, cucumber, mint, carrot, green onions, bell pepper and nuts. Add the fresh squeezed lime juice and toss again.

4. Plate the salad and add the ground turkey to the top of it. Serve with fresh lime wedges.

*If you want it completely sugar free, substitute stevia for the coconut sugar.

TURKEY BREAKFAST HASH

This is a quick easy protein packed dish. I usually make my own pico de gallo but feel free to use a jared salsa that you enjoy and that is gsdf. Another tasty way to make this dish is to add diced sweet potatoes to the cooked ground turkey. A perfect one pot dish for breakfast or dinner.

SERVES: 4; PREP TIME: 10 MINS; COOK TIME: 15 MINS

Ingredients

- 1 lb. organic ground turkey
- 1 cup salsa of choice
- 6 eggs
- 2 tablespoons chopped cilantro
- 1 tablespoon coconut oil
- ½ teaspoon salt
- few grinds of fresh black pepper
- ¼ teaspoon ground cumin

Directions

1. In a large skillet over medium high heat, melt the coconut oil. Add the ground turkey and cook all the way through (4-5 minutes) breaking it up with a spatula as it cooks.

2. Add the salsa, salt, pepper and ground cumin and cook over medium low heat for 3 minutes.

3. Crack the eggs gently into the mix and cover. Cook until eggs are done 5-7 minutes.

4. Top with chopped cilantro..

TURKEY CABBAGE ROLLS

These tasty turkey cabbage rolls are a hearty dish and perfect with a side salad. The rolls are baked in marinara sauce. The stuffing has turkey, garlic, spinach, onion and Italian seasonings. You can make this a day ahead and bake right before you are ready to eat. This dish freezes very well also.

SERVES: 4; PREP TIME: 25 MINS; COOK TIME: 60 MINS

TURKEY FLORENTINE STUFFED CABBAGE ROLLS

Ingredients

- 1 pound ground turkey
- ½ yellow onion, diced
- 2 cloves of garlic, minced
- 4 cups of baby spinach
- 8 ounces of mushrooms, diced small
- 1 head of green cabbage
- ¼ teaspoon dried basil
- ¼ teaspoon dried oregano
- ½ teaspoon salt
- ¼ teaspoon ground pepper
- 2 tablespoons coconut oil, divided
- 2 cups marinara sauce

Directions

1. Preheat oven to 350 degrees F.

2. In a large skillet over medium high heat, melt one tablespoon coconut oil. Add the onion, garlic and cook for 2-3 minutes until translucent. (Don't burn the garlic) Add the spinach and cook for 2 minutes turning gently with tongs. Set aside to cool

3. In a clean skillet, over medium high heat, melt the coconut oil and then add the mushrooms. Sauté until thoroughly cooked, about 5-7 minutes. Set aside to cool.

4. Fill a soup pot with water and bring it up to boil.

5. Cut the core out of the cabbage. Put the entire head in the boiling water. Using tongs, pull the outside leaf off and remove from water after about 2 minutes. Then remove the next one. They will be moveable as they cook. Let them cool.

6. Chop the spinach, onion, garlic mixture up and put into a large bowl. Add the mushrooms, turkey, oregano, basil, salt, pepper and ½ cup marinara to the bowl. Using your fingers mix gently.

7. Cut the rib section out of every cabbage leaf, the bottom thick part. Lay flat on cutting board.

8. Pour ½ cup marinara into a 9" x 13" baking dish.

9. Place ⅓ cup of the turkey mix into the center of each cabbage leaf. Then fold the leaf over the turkey mature and place seam side down in the baking dish.

10. Pour the remaining 1 ½ cups marinara sauce evenly over top of the cabbage rolls. Cover with foil and bake for 1 hour. Serve the cabbage rolls with the sauce spooned over.

TURKEY CHILI

This turkey chili is a quick dish to make and packed full of flavor from the onion, garlic, jalapeños, fire roasted tomatoes and seasonings. It is a versatile dish that you can eat in a bowl or wrap up with lettuce leaves. I actually love to put it warm over shredded romaine and cabbage with a squeeze of lime on top.

SERVES: 4; PREP TIME: 10 MINS; COOK TIME: 50 MINS

Ingredients

- 1 pound ground turkey
- 1 small yellow onion, diced
- 2 cloves garlic, minced
- 2 jalapeños, seeded and minced
- 1 15 ounce can fire roasted tomatoes
- 1 15 ounce can black beans, drained and rinsed
- 1 cup of stock
- 2 teaspoons ground cumin
- 2 teaspoons ground chili powder
- 1 teaspoon oregano
- ½ teaspoon salt
- 2 tablespoons coconut oil, divided
- 2 tablespoons fresh cilantro, chopped

Directions

1. Heat a large skillet over medium high heat and melt the coconut oil. Add the onion and cook until translucent 6-8 minutes. Add the garlic and jalapeños and cook 2 more minutes.

2. Add the turkey, cumin, chili powder, oregano and salt. Cook while breaking up the meat with a spatula until done, about 7-8 minutes.

3. Add black beans, fire roasted tomatoes and the broth. Bring up to boil. Then lower the heat simmer, stirring occasionally 23-30 minutes. Serve and top with cilantro.

TURKEY FRIED RICE

This dish works best with left over rice that is cold so as it heats it can soak up all the flavor of the fresh ginger, garlic, coconut amino and the vinegar. You can substitute brown rice for cauliflower rice. Just cook the cauliflower rice with the veggies and seasonings. Delicious as a one dish meal or put in lettuce leaves.

SERVES: 4

Ingredients

- 1 cup brown rice (cooked ahead of time)
- ½ pound ground turkey
- 2-3 cloves garlic, minced
- 2-inch of fresh ginger, peeled and grated
- 1 cup frozen peas
- 3 carrots cut into small square pieces
- 1 cup snow peas, halved
- 1 cup purple cabbage, shredded
- 1 bell pepper, cut into thin strips
- 2 tablespoons coconut oil
- 2 tablespoons rice vinegar
- 3 tablespoons coconut aminos or tamari
- 4 green onions, sliced thin

Directions

1. Heat a large skillet over medium high heat and melt the coconut oil. Add the turkey, garlic and ginger to the pan. Using a spatula to break up the meat while cooking it all the way through 5-8 minutes.

2. Add all of the veggies, rice, seasonings and mix while cooking over medium high heat for 4-6 minutes. Top with the green onions.

TURKEY MEATBALLS IN THAI INSPIRED SAUCE

Turkey meatballs in Thai Coconut Sauce is a perfect recipe if you are cutting down on read meat but still want a hearty dish. The spice of the red curry, ginger, garlic and green onions flavor the balls themselves. They also have shredded zucchini to add moisture. They are browned and set int a red curry to simmer and cook through. I love to serve this with a sprinkle of fresh cilantro and a squeeze of fresh lime to make the flavors bright.

SERVES: 4 - 6; PREP TIME: 20 MINS; COOK TIME: 25 MINS

Ingredients

FOR THE MEATBALLS:

- 2 pounds ground turkey
- 1 cup zucchini, shredded & liquid squeezed out
- 4 green onions, white and green part finely chopped
- 12 fresh basil leaves, finely chopped
- 2 inch piece of ginger, grated
- 3 garlic cloves, finely minced
- 2 teaspoons red curry paste

FOR THE SAUCE:

- 1 ½ cups coconut milk
- 3 tablespoons tomato paste
- 2 teaspoons red curry paste
- juice of a lime
- 2 tablespoons coconut oil
- ½ bunch fresh cilantro, chopped
- 2 limes, quartered

Directions

1. In a large bowl, add the ground turkey, zucchini, green onions, basil leaves, ginger, garlic and red curry paste. Gently mix with your fingers. Divide the mix into quarters. Roll 6 meatballs from each section so that they are all similar size. Set aside.

2. In a bowl mix together the coconut milk, tomato paste, red curry paste and the juice of a lime. Set aside.

3. In a large skillet on medium high heat, melt the coconut oil. Add the meatballs and cook until light brown on the outside, turning them gently for 5-7 minutes. They will finish cooking in the sauce. Drain any grease off.

4. Pour the sauce over the meatballs, lower the heat to low, cover and cook 15 minutes or until done.

5. Serve the meatballs in bowls with the sauce, sprinkle the cilantro over and add a squeeze of lime if desired. May also be served over rice.

TURKEY MEATLOAF

This turkey meatloaf is packed with flavor from the onion, carrot garlic and spinach which also helps keep the meatloaf moist. It cooks up quickly and is also very good left over.

SERVES: 4; PREP TIME: 15 MINS; COOK TIME: 35 MINS

Ingredients

- 1 ½ pounds ground turkey
- ¼ cup gf bread crumbs
- 1 large egg
- ½ yellow onion, grated
- 2 cloves garlic, minced
- 1 carrot, grated or chopped fine
- ½ cup cooked spinach, chopped
- ½ teaspoon oregano
- ½ teaspoon salt
- ¼ teaspoon black pepper
- ¼ cup ketchup

Directions

1. Heat oven to 450° F.
2. In a large bowl, gently combine all the ingredients.
3. Form the mixture into a loaf and put in a baking dish, topping with ketchup.
4. Cook 30-35 minutes until done. Let stand 5 minutes before serving so the juices distribute..

TURKEY QUINOA CASSEROLE

This turkey quinoa casserole is inspired by the flavors of Italy. Wine, garlic, onions, basil and tomatoes make this something special. I like to make it ahead of time and then bake to warm it up right before dinner. Leftovers freeze well also. If you want it a little more rich flavored, feel free to add some vegan cheese or some cashew cream to the quinoa mix.

SERVES: 4; PREP TIME: 15 MINS; COOK TIME: 30 MINS

Ingredients

- 1 pound ground turkey
- 2 cups cooked quinoa (make ahead)
- ½ yellow onion, diced
- 2 cloves garlic, minced
- 1 cup cooked spinach
- ½ cup white wine or stock
- ½ teaspoon red pepper flakes
- ½ teaspoon dried oregano
- ½ teaspoon dried basil
- 4-6 Roma tomatoes sliced
- 12 basil leaves, cut into strips
- 1 tablespoon coconut oil

Directions

1. Preheat oven to 400 degrees F.

2. In a large skillet, melt the coconut oil over medium high heat and then add the turkey, onion, salt and pepper flakes. Cooking it all the way through, breaking up the chunks with your spatula, 5-7 minutes.

3. Add garlic, spinach, and wine to the skillet. Bring to a simmer, stirring frequently.

4. Stir in cooked quinoa, dried oregano and dried basil Reduce heat to medium and cook until heated through, 3-5 minutes.

5. Transfer quinoa mixture to a 9" x 13" baking dish.

6. Arrange slices of tomato in a layer over the quinoa. Bake in preheated oven for 15 minutes and then top with the fresh basil leaves..

TURKEY SHEPHERD'S PIE

Shepherd's pie is a great one dish meal. I like to make these on the weekends and bake for a hearty dinner mid week. Left overs freeze well also. I love the flavor of fresh rosemary and garlic with the turkey in this dish. It makes it special.

SERVES: 2; PREP TIME: 15 MINS; COOK TIME: 30 MINS

Ingredients

- 1 pound ground turkey
- 3 carrots, peeled and diced
- ½ yellow onion, diced
- 2 cloves garlic, minced
- 1 cup frozen peas, defrosted
- 1 cup frozen pearl onions, defrosted
- 2 medium sweet potatoes, peeled, cut into chunks
- 8 ounces of mushrooms, sliced
- ½ cup chicken stock
- 1 teaspoon salt, divided
- 2 teaspoons fresh rosemary, chopped
- 1 teaspoon dried thyme
- ½ teaspoon cinnamon
- fresh black pepper to taste

Directions

1. Preheat oven to 400 degrees F.

2. In a large pot, put the sweet potatoes and cover with cold water. Bring to boil and cook until fork tender 20-30 minutes. Drain, mash with the cinnamon. Set aside.

3. In a large skillet, heat the coconut oil over medium heat. Add carrots, mushrooms and onions and cook until soft, about 5 minutes.

4. Add turkey, diced onion and garlic and cook, breaking up meat with a spatula, until cooked through 5-7 minutes.

5. Add the peas, pearl onions, rosemary, thyme, salt and pepper. Mix well. Add the stock and simmer until liquid reduces, 10 minutes.

6. Pour this mixture into a baking dish. Top with the sweet potatoes. Bake 25 minutes.

TURKEY SPAGHETTI SAUCE

This sauce has an all day simmer flavor but cooks in under an hour. A very tasty way to make a quick meal. I like to use the baby bella mushrooms in this dish since they have a deeper mushroom flavor.

SERVES: 4 -6; PREP TIME: 10 MINS; COOK TIME: 45 MINS

Ingredients

- 1 pound ground turkey
- 1 yellow onion, diced
- 4 cloves garlic, minced
- 1 large carrot, grated and chopped
- 8 ounces mushrooms, sliced
- 1 28-ounce can crushed tomatoes
- 1 cup red wine (stock can be substituted)
- ½ teaspoon dried oregano
- ½ teaspoon dried basil
- ½ teaspoon salt
- fresh black pepper
- pinch red chili flakes
- 1 tablespoon coconut oil

Directions

1. In a medium dutch oven, add the coconut oil and melt over medium high heat. Add the onion, garlic and carrot, cook 3 minutes stirring.

2. Add the turkey and cook until done, 5-6 minutes. Add the mushrooms, crushed tomatoes, red

wine, oregano, basil, slat, pepper and chili flakes and stir. Bring up to a bubble and then simmer for 45 minutes.

3. Serve over spaghetti squash, zucchini noodles or gluten free noodles.

TURKEY STUFFED PEPPERS

These stuffed peppers are an easy dish to make and tasty to eat. I loved stuffed peppers because it is a meal in a pepper! I love left overs for lunch the next day.

SERVES:4; PREP TIME: 10 MINS; COOK TIME: 50 MINS

Ingredients

- 1 pound ground turkey
- 4 bell peppers, tops, seeds and veins removed
- ½ yellow onion, diced
- 2 cloves garlic, minced
- 1 cup brown rice (made ahead of time)
- ½ teaspoon dried oregano
- ½ teaspoon dried basil
- ½ teaspoon salt
- 4 cups baby spinach
- 11/2 cups marinara sauce
- 1 tablespoon coconut

Directions

1. Preheat oven to 375 degrees F.

2. In a large skillet over medium-high heat, melt the coconut oil. Add the turkey, onion, garlic, oregano, basil and salt. Cook while using a spatula to break up clumps 5-7 minutes. Put in a bowl and set aside.

3. In a clean skillet over medium high heat, cook the spinach and then drain. Add to the bowl with the turkey. Add ½ cup marinara to the mix and mix well.

4. Spoon mixture into hollowed peppers, put into a baking dish. Pour the marinara sauce over. Bake until peppers are tender 30-40 minutes.

TURKEY STUFFED PORTABELLAS

This is a fantastic tasting dish and very hearty. The meatiness of the mushrooms stuffed with eh turkey, spinach and seasonings make this a go to easy dish! I love to have a crispy side salad next to it.

SERVES: 4; PREP TIME: 15 MINS; COOK TIME: 30 MINS

Ingredients

- 4 large portobello mushroom caps, gills removed
- ½ pound ground turkey
- 1 yellow onion, diced
- 2 cloves garlic, minced
- 2 cups baby spinach
- ½ can fire roasted tomatoes
- ½ teaspoon dried oregano
- ½ teaspoon dried basil
- ½ teaspoon salt
- fresh black pepper to taste
- 2 tablespoons coconut oil, divided

Directions

1. Pre heat oven to 450 F.
2. Clean the mushrooms using a spoon to gently scrape out the gills. Brush the caps with 1

tablespoon coconut oil, place on baking sheet and bake gill side down for 20 minutes. Let cool.

3. In a large skillet over medium high heat, melt 1 tablespoon coconut oil. Add the onion and sauté for 3 minutes.

4. Add the turkey, garlic, oregano, basil, salt and pepper and cook while using a spatula to break up the chunks, 5-7 minutes. Add the spinach and fire roasted tomatoes, and stir together. Let cool to room temp.

5. Flip the mushrooms over and stuff with the turkey mix. Bake 15 minutes.

6. These can be made ahead, kept in the fridge and then baked for 25 minutes.

VEGGIE TURKEY QUINOA

SERVES: 4; PREP TIME: 10 MINS; COOK TIME: 20 MINS

Ingredients

- 1 pound ground turkey
- 1 yellow onion, sliced thin
- 16 ounces of mushrooms, cut into slices
- 4 tightly packed cups baby spinach leaves
- 6 roma tomatoes, diced
- 1 bell pepper, cut into thin strips
- 2 cloves garlic minced
- ½ cup dry white wine (can use chicken stock)
- ½ teaspoon salt
- fresh black pepper
- ½ teaspoon dried basil
- ½ teaspoon dried thyme
- pinch red peper flakes
- 2 tablespoons coconut oil
- 1 lemon
- 3 cups cooked quinoa

Directions

1. In a large skillet, melt 1 tablespoon coconut oil over medium high heat. Add the turkey, onions, salt, pepper, basil, oregano and red pepper lakes. Using a spatula or wooden spoon cook turkey mixture, breaking up the big chunks. Cook until

cooked through 4-5 minutes. Remove and set aside.

2. Add 1 tablespoon coconut oil to pan, the mushrooms and dried thyme. Cook until they are brown, 3-5 minutes. .

3. Add tomatoes, garlic, bell pepper and spinach and cook until spinach is wilted. Add the turkey mixture and the wine or stock to the pan, stir well. Cook for 3 minutes over medium high heat.

4. Add the quinoa and the juice of the lemon, stir well and cook until heated through 3-4 minutes.

WINGS

BALSAMIC CHICKEN WINGS

When I was young, my grandfather let me watch football with him. He watched all of the college games and the professional ones. He explained the game to me. I just liked getting to spend time with him. One year he and my grandmother took me to my first college game. We had great seats and it was so exciting. On a nice football Sunday I love to nibble on chicken wings. I wanted to create a deeper flavor than the normal hot wings. The vinegar, honey and soy create a sweet sticky glaze to the wings. The garlic brings a bit of zing to the mix. I like to brush the marinade over the wings a few times before they are done to get a stronger flavor from the glaze.

SERVES: 1 - 2; PREP TIME: 5 MINS; COOK TIME: 30 MINS; MARINADE TIME: 1 HOUR

Ingredients

- 1 pound chicken wings
- 2 cloves garlic minced
- 2 tablespoons soy sauce
- ¼ cup balsamic vinegar
- 2 tablespoons honey

Directions

1. In a bowl mix together vinegar, garlic, honey and soy sauce. Rinse and dry chicken wings. Place in a plastic zip bag. Pour sauce over wings making sure to coat them all over. Seal the bag and place in the refrigerator for one hour.

2. Remove the chicken wings from the bag and place on a foil lined cookie sheet. Bake 375° for 30 minutes.

Serving Suggestions: For variety add 1 teaspoon red chili flakes for heat. Brush marinade over wings after 15 minutes of cooking for a more intense flavor.

HONEY GARLIC WINGS

Finger licking good wings. Flavors of honey, garlic and a touch of heat make these wings disappear fast!

SERVES: 4; PREP TIME: 15 MINS; COOK TIME: 50 - 60 MINS

Ingredients

- 2 pounds of chicken wings
- ½ cup of honey
- 6 garlic cloves, minced
- 1 tablespoon coconut oil, melted
- ½ teaspoon salt
- fresh black pepper
- ½ teaspoon cayenne chili powder

Directions

1. Preheat the oven to 400 degrees

2. With a knife, separate the flappers from the drumetts and cut the wing tips off and discard.

3. In a large bowl, mix the rest of the ingredients. Add the chicken pieces and coat well.

4. Put chicken on racks that are on top of sheet pans so that the hot air circulates around the wings.

5. Bake 50-60 minutes until done..

SPICY HONEY MUSTARD CHICKEN WINGS

These wings disappeared from the plate Thursday night while watching pre-season football! They are a little messy but worth the mess! They come out spicy, tangy, sweet and delicious. Chicken wings and football is one of my favorite combinations so I like a variety of wings. This one is a sure winner.

SERVES: 4; PREP TIME: 10 MINS; COOK TIME: 40 MINS

Ingredients

- 2 pounds chicken wings, flats and drummy seperated
- ½ cup local raw organic honey
- ⅓ cup Dijon mustard
- 2 tablespoons bourbon
- 1 ½ tablespoons tamari or coconut aminos
- ½ teaspoon red pepper flakes
- ¼ teaspoon salt
- 2 teaspoons sriracha (add more for more heat)
- 1 ½ tablespoons coconut oil

Directions

1. Pre heat oven to 400 degrees F.

2. In a medium size sauce pan, add all the ingredients and simmer while constantly stirring for 3 minutes.

3. Put the wings on a cooling rack on top of a large baking sheet. Spreading them out so that the air can circulate around them.

4. Put into oven cook 20 minutes, flip them over and another 20 minutes. they should be nice and golden.

5. You can put them under the broiler at this point for a few moments to make them a little more crispy.

VINEGAR CHILE CHICKEN WINGS

These chicken wings turn out sweet, spicy and tangy. Marinade them over night for the best flavor. You can either grill them the next day or bake them in the oven. These wings are a great snack on game day! Even cold the next day they are wonderful.

SERVES: 4; PREP TIME: 10 MINS; COOK TIME: 45 MINS

Ingredients

- 2 pounds chicken wings, tips removed and flats and drumettes separated
- ½ cup rice vinegar
- 2 tablespoons coconut oil
- 7 cloves of garlic, smashed
- 1 teaspoon red chili flakes
- 1 tablespoon honey
- 1 teaspoon salt
- 2 limes
- 2 teaspoons cumin
- 1 teaspoon hot chili powder

Directions

1. In a large zip plastic bag add the chilies, vinegar, coconut oil, garlic and salt to the bag. Shake to mix well.

2. Add the chicken wings to the bag and make sure every one gets coated with the marinade. Set in fridge over night.

3. Pre heat oven to 375 f or the bbq.

4. Remove wings from bag and pat dry.

5. In a bowl add 1 tablespoon coconut oil,cumin and chili powder, mix well.

6. Toss the wings in this mix and either bbq or lay on baking racks on baking sheets.

7. If cooking on BBQ: cook 15-20 minutes turning half way through.

8. If cooking in oven: bake 40-45 minutes turning half way through.

9. Plate and then zest the zest of one lime over the wings and squeeze the juice of both limes over the wings.

10. Serve and enjoy!

CPSIA information can be obtained
at www.ICGtesting.com
Printed in the USA
LVOW13s2031070317

526429LV00021B/479/P